E. N. (Edmund Needham) Morrill

History and statistics of Brown County, Kansas

From its earliest settlement to the present time

E. N. (Edmund Needham) Morrill

History and statistics of Brown County, Kansas
From its earliest settlement to the present time

ISBN/EAN: 9783741182747

Manufactured in Europe, USA, Canada, Australia, Japa

Cover: Foto ©ninafisch / pixelio.de

Manufactured and distributed by brebook publishing software (www.brebook.com)

E. N. (Edmund Needham) Morrill

History and statistics of Brown County, Kansas

HISTORY AND STATISTICS

OF

BROWN CO., KANSAS,

FROM

ITS EARLIEST SETTLEMENT TO THE PRESENT TIME,

EMBRACING

*INCIDENTS AND HARDSHIPS OF PIONEER LIFE, THE RISE
AND PROGRESS MADE IN TWENTY-TWO YEARS,
LOCATION, RESOURCES, FERTILITY
OF ITS SOIL, ETC., ETC.*

COMPILED BY

MAJ. E. N. MORRILL.

HIAWATHA, KANSAS.
KANSAS HERALD BOOK, NEWS AND JOB OFFICE.
JULY 4TH, 1876.

HISTORY.

On the 30th day of May, 1854, the Act of Congress providing for a territorial organization of the Territories of Kansas and Nebraska, was signed by President Pierce, and became a law, and the large amount of public lands embraced within their boundaries was thrown open to settlement under the pre-emption laws of the United States. Under the provisions of that Act an election was held on the 30th of March, 1855, to choose members of the first Legislature of the Territory of Kansas. The Legislature thus elected met at Pawnee and soon after adjourned to meet at Shawnee Manual Labor School on the 22nd of July of the same year. At this session of the Legislature an act was passed, districting a portion of the territory into counties and naming the counties thus laid off. This act provides that Browne county shall be bounded as follows: Beginning at the southwest corner of Doniphan county, thence west twenty-four miles, thence south thirty miles, thence east to the west line of Atchison county, thence north to the northwest corner of Atchison county, thence east with said line of Atchison county, to the northwest corner of Doniphan county, thence north with said west line of Doniphan county to place of beginning. It will be observed that two serious mistakes occur in this description—at the commencement it should be northwest corner of Doniphan county, and near the close it should be southwest corner of Doniphan county. The same act attached the County of Browne to the County of Doniphan for civil and military purposes. In regard to the origin of the name, there seems to be quite a difference of opinion. The Secretary of the State Board of Agriculture, Hon. Alfred Gray, in his report for 1875, says Brown county was was named in honor of Hon. Albert G. Brown of Mississippi, who was a member of the United States Senate at the time of the passage of the act organizing Kansas Territory. In support of this view, a letter from Judge F. G. Adams, an old and honored citizen of the State is herewith submitted.

"TOPEKA, KAN., April 6, 1876.
Hon. Alfred Grey. Sec'y State Board of Agriculture:

Dear Sir:—You have shown me the letter of Hon. E. N. Morrill, in which he expresses a doubt as to the correctness of your Fourth Annual Report, in respect to the origin of the name of Brown county.

I furnished you the information for the item in your report upon the authority of Hon. John Martin, of Topeka, who was a clerk in the legislature during which the county was originally established and named—the session of 1855—the first territorial session, held at Shawnee Mission, in Johnson county.

Mr. Martin's recollection was quite clear on the point, and his information was so explicit that I had no doubt of its correctness. Since seeing Major Morrill's letter to you, I have made further inquiry on the subject of Mr. Alex. S. Johnson and Mr. H. D. McMeekin, of this city, both of whom were members of that first Territorial legislature. They fully agreed with Mr. Martin, that the county was named in honor of Albert G. Brown, of Mississippi, as stated in your report.

In respect to the orthography of the name, I have examined, and find the following facts:

The act of 1855, 'defining the boundaries of the counties, of Kansas,' gives the spelling Browne. It is so in the published statutes and journals, and so in the enrolled bill preserved in the Secretary of State's office.

But it does not so occur in the enrolled bills of the second session of the Legislature, held in 1857, commencing at Lecompton, Jan. 4th of that year. In the enrolled bills of that second session the final e is dropped from Brown county. This is so in an act redefining the boundaries of the several counties of the Territory, and the same is true as to all of the enrolled bills of that session, including one redistricting the Territory for legislative purposes. But in the published statutes of that session, 1857, the name is invariably printed with the final e—following the statutes of 1845.

The enrolled bill is the highest authority of variance like this. It was then the legislature of 1857 that changed the orthography from Browne to Brown. The latter orthography has since been followed in Kansas statutes.

Major Morrill was a member of the House of Representatives at the third legislative session, and the first page of the House journal of that session shows that he appeared as the member from the fourth and fifth districts, embracing Brown and Nemaha counties—the final e being omitted in the Journal as in all the laws and proceedings of that session.

Albert G. Brown's name was not spelled with a final e. If, then, Messrs. Johnson, Martin and McMeekin are correct, as they doubtless are, in their recollection, that the legislature of 1855 intended to honor the Mississippi Senator, by giving his name to the county, a clerical error was made in the enrollment of the bill—an error which went into the printed statutes of that and the succeeding sessions, and so into the early records of the county. There was no member of the legislature from Doniphan named Brown, nor from that part of the Territory, during these early sessions. Brown was attached to Doniphan at the first session, and detached at the second. In the act detaching, it was named Brown without the e.

The legislature, at its second session, was pro-slavery;

and could not, in dropping the e, have made the change for the purpose of honoring old John Brown. No formal act in regard to the name was ever passed, other than those of the two pro-slavery legislatures. The succeeding legislatures, in acts in which the same occurs, have simply followed the orthography fixed by the acts of 1857.

It is not singular that Major Morrill should have fallen into error in this matter. Doubtless he had not, at the time, taken notice of the precise facts. John Brown's "trail" crossed Brown county. It is a settled tradition in that section that the county was named after the old martyr. It gives me no pleasure to dispel the error.

Yours, F. G Adams,
Sec. State Hist. Society."

This seems improbable, for in the act defining the the boundaries, the name is spelled with a final e ; and in the laws of that session as well as in the laws of the pro-slavery legislature of 1857, it is, without exception, spelled with the terminal e. It seems hardly reasonable to suppose that a legislative body desiring to honor a distinguished man by giving to a new county his name would fail to follow his orthography in the spelling of that name. Among the early settlers of the county it was generally reported and universally accepted as a fact, that the county was named in honor of O. H. Browne, a prominent member of the legislature of 1855, who represented Douglas county. In support of this side of the question, the following letters are given from influential members of that legislature, now living in the State. J. H. Stringfellow, of Atchison, writes the Champion as follows :

"Mr. Editor :—In a communication some short time since in your valuable paper from Judge F. G. Adams, who is usually so correct, there is an error regarding the name of Brown county, which should be corrected, as it is likely to become a part of the future history of Kansas. I am not surprised that the facts have become confused, as so long a time has elapsed, and such tremendous events have intervened since their occurrence. The name of the county was originally Browne, after a very brilliant and very eccentric member of the House at the time, O. H. Browne, of the then Third Representative District, and a resident of what is now Douglas county, where he died some few years since. There were several counties named after members of the one or the other of the two houses, viz., Johnson, after Rev. Thos. Johnson, a member of the Council ; Lykins, after Rev. David Lykins, of the Council, an ex-Indian missionary ; Coffey, after A. M. Coffey, of the Council from Kentucky ; Anderson, after Joseph C. Anderson, of the House ; Marshall, after F. I. Marshall, of the House.

Of the above gentlemen, I think only two are now living—F. I. Marshall, now of Colorado, an enterprising, intelligent man, and highly respected ; and J. C. Anderson, now, I think, of Kentucky, a very intelligent lawyer, and all of them men of unblemished personal character.

J. H. STRINGFELLOW,
Atchison, Kan."

Col. T. W. Waterson also adds his testimony in the same direction.

"Marysville, Kan., June 28, 1876.

HON. E. N. MORRILL :—Dear sir.—Yours of the 26th inst. came to hand last evening. In reply I would say that my recollection is very clear that the origin and reason of your county being called Browne was, that a man by the name of O. H. Browne was a member of the legislature at that time, and was very desirous of having a county called for him, as were a good many other members. For instance, Marshall, Richardson, Johnson, Coffey, Lykins, etc., were all named after members. If this does not cover the ground, please let me hear from you and I will try and give all the information I can.

Yours Truly, THOS. W. WATERSON."

Honorable John A. Halderman, of Leavenworth, also a member of the first Legislature, writes : "My recollection is that Browne county was called for O. H. Browne, a member of the first House of Representatives, who died, a few years since, in Osage; and not for Hon. A. G. Brown, of Mississippi."

This would seem to prove conclusively that the intention of the first legislature was to honor one of their members by giving his name to this county. Why the final e was subsequently dropped does not appear; but as the name is spellled Browne wherever it appears in the laws enacted by the pro-slavery legislatures and Brown in all the laws enacted by Free-state legislatures, it is fair to presume that the name was changed for political reasons.

In the early records of Doniphan county the following entries are found pertaining to Browne county. At a meeting of the commissioners of Doniphan county, on Monday, the 17th day of Sept., A. D. 1855, it was ordered that the county of Browne be and it is hereby organized as a municipal township to be known as Browne county township.

Ordered. That the Territorial election for Delegate to the next Congress of the United States be held at the house of W. C. Foster, on the SouthFork of the Nemaha for the county of Browne and that Wm. C. Foster, Wm. Purket and E. W. Short be appointed judges to hold the same.

Ordered, That a vote of the people be taken on the day of the territorial election authorizing the county court to grant or withhold license for the retail of ardent spirits in each township. It may be printed or written on each ticket, License, or No License.

Ordered, That John C. Boggs and Wm. C. Foster be appointed Justices of the Peace, and that Wm. Purket be appointed Constable for the county of Brown, in the territory of Kansas, for, and during the term prescribed by law and until their successors are duly elected and qualified. At the January term, 1856, the following orders were passed. Ordered that John W. Smith be and he is hereby appointed assessor of Brown and Doniphan counties for and during the term prescribed by law and until his successor is elected and qualified; and that he be requested to enter into bond to the Territory of Kansas in the penal sum of FOUR HUNDRED DOLLARS conditioned for the faithful performance of the duties of his office. Ordered, That A. Hays be and he is hereby appointed special Marshal to take the census of Doniphan and Brown counties during the term prescribed by law.

June 16, 1856, the following orders were entered. Ordered, That the account filed with the clerk of this court by Henry Adams and R. L. Kirk, commissioners to locate a Territorial road from Atchison to Marysville, amounting to one hundred and four dollars and twenty-five cents against Brown county for surveying said road through said county be and the same is hereby audited and allowed against said county; and that the clerk of this Tribunal be and he is hereby authorized to issue warrants on Brown county and in favor of the several persons whose names are mentioned in the account. Ordered, That the court will not allow the items in the above account for use of tent and cooking utensils and provisions, amounting to $12.93.

Here follows a long report of the road commissioners of the road above referred to.

July 22, 1856, an order was passed directing the county surveyor to survey and mark out the boundary line between Brown and Doniphan counties. On the 16th of Sept., 1856, several orders were passed pertaining to Brown county. Among them was one that the assessor should file seperate bills for assessing against Doniphan and Brown counties and his assessment rolls should be received provided that pre-emption claims and shares in joint stock companies not incorporated shall not be taxed. It was also ordered that township ranges numbered 15 and 16 in Brown county be and they are hereby constituted a municipal township, to be known as Walnut township; and that an election for members to the next legislative assembly of the Territory of Kansas, to be held at the house of W. C. Foster, in said township, on the 1st Monday in October next, and that W. C. Foster, ———— and ———— be and they are hereby appointed judges to hold said election. Ordered that township ranges 17 and 18 be and they are hereby constituted a municipal township to be known as Mission township and that an election for members of the next Legislative assembly of the Territory of Kansas be held at the house of Henry Smith, on the 1st Monday of October next, within and for said township, and that Henry Smith, ——— Thompson and James Smith be and they are hereby appointed judges to the same. Ordered that the rate of tax for county purposes for Brown county for the present year shall be fifty cents for each poll and one-sixth of one per cent on all other taxable property. On the 17th of Nov., 1856, the the account of John W. Smith for assessing Brown county was allowed, amounting to $48. The foregoing, with the exception of a few orders pertaining to road and personal matters, seem to be all the orders of the commissioners of Doniphan county relating to Brown county business.

On page 44 of laws of 1857, the boundaries of the county are again given, correcting the errors in the laws of 1855, and the name is still spelled with an e. On page 84 of the same session laws is an act approved Feb. —, which reads as folllows: That the county of Browne, which is attached to the county of Doniphan is hereby detached from said county of Doniphan. That Claytonville be the temporary seat of justice of Browne county. That at the first general election there shall be three commissioners elected, who shall, after first taking an oath, etc., proceed to locate the permanent seat of justice. That the present legislature of the Territory of Kansas shall elect a Probate Judge, Sheriff and two commissioners for Browne county, who shall hold their offices until the general election in October, 1857, and until their successors are elected and qualified. During the same session of the legislature Geo. E. Clayton was elected Probate Judge of Browne county—the Probate Judge being, under the then existing law, chairman of the county commissioners court. Henry Smith and D. M. Lochnane were elected commissioners, but as Mr. Lochnane was not a resident of the county at the time, this left a vacancy in the board which was not, however, filled. Pettus Thompson was elected Sheriff, but he declined the office and did not qualify. The court thus constituted formally organized and held a session at Claytonville on the 16th day of March, 1857, in a small log house which is still standing and which now forms a part of the residence of O. C. Whitney, Esq. This was the first court ever held in Brown county, and this log hut was the first court house. The first act of the court was to appoint James Waterson clerk. James A. Fulton was appointed Sheriff, but later in the day this appointment was for some reason rescinded and at the following session he was again appointed. John Dunbar was appointed Treasurer and E. M. Hubbard, Coroner. Dunbar probably declined to act, as at the next session of the court Richard L. Oldham was appointed Treasurer. The court then divided the county into four municipal townships, nearly equal in extent of territory, naming the N. E. township Irving, the S. E. Claytonville, the S. W. Lochnane and the N. W. Walnut Creek. Lra H. Smith was appointed county surveyor but he refused to accept any appointment at the hands of this court, holding that the legislature that provided for the organization of the county was forced upon the territory by fraud and violence. Joseph A. Brown was appointed assessor and M. C. Willis, Justice of the Peace. At the next session of this court, held March 31, 1857, it was ordered that John H. Whitehead have a license to sell intoxicating liquors at his store in Kinnekuk for six months from April 1, 1857, upon payment of $25. As Kinnekuk was just over the line in Atchison county and entirely beyond the jurisdiction of this tribunal, it was evidently a clear gain of $25 to the county. At the same session of the court it was ordered that $500 be appropriated for the building of a court house on the north square in Claytonville, said house to be a frame 30 feet long and 20 feet wide and to be enclosed by 1st of June, 1857. Richard L. Oldham was appointed commissioner to build this house. A tax levy was made at this session of one-sixth of one per cent for county purposes, and one-sixth of one per cent for building purposes. Under an act of the pro-slavery legislature all persons who settled upon secs. 16 and 36 (school land) before the survey of the public lands, were required to prove their settlement before the county court and pay to the county Treasurer $1.25 per acre for such lands—the money thus received to be made a permanent school fund. Quite a number of the early settlers of the county—M. L. Sawin, Thomas Brigham, John Page, Jos. Farron, Ely Corneilison, F. M. Starns, Isaac H. Barkley and Nathaniel Kimberlin proved their settlement before the county court but the U. S. Government refused to recognize this disposition of the lands and required the parties to prove their settlement at the U. S. Land Office, treating these lands as Government lands and not school lands. At the session of this court held May 18, 1857, E. H. Niles, Thurston Chase, Noah Hanson and others petitioned to have school districts organized in town 2, range 16. This seems to be the first action ever taken in the county towards organizing school districts and came from a section of the county which for many years took the lead in educational matters. The next day a petition was presented from the settlers' in town 3, range 18 to have that township organized into school districts. The records fail to show who the petitioners were. At this time voting precincts were established for the county, at house of W. C. Foster, for Walnut Creek township; at house of J. B. Heaton, at Mt. Roy, for Irving township; at house of C. W. Magill, for Lochnane township; and at hotel in Claytonville for that township.

Lewis Dunn was appointed Justice of the Peace at this session. Petitions for roads were presented and necessary action taken to establish them at each session of the commissioners' court during the whole year of 1857. At the next session of the court, held July 20, Leander Sawyer and John G. Spencer were appointed Justices of the Peace. The Sheriff of the county, who was, by virtue of his office, collector of taxes, submitted a report for the year 1856, a copy of which is herewith given in full.

Brown Co., Kansas Territory:
                In acc't with James A. Fulton.
        1857.   Collector of said county.
Cr.   By the tax book of 1856 $106.41
    "   J. H. Whitehead's license   25.00
    "   G. W. Williams'   "   -   25.00
                                        _____
                                         $156.41
Dr.   To per centage for collecting revenue $7.40
    "   "   "   "   "   License 1.00
                                              _____
                                               $8.40

Of the above account there is due to John W. Smith, Assessor of Brown county.   - $38.60

There is lost of the revenue of the county by error of the assessor assessing persons out of the county and delinquent as per my return $69.51

And there is in my hands, belonging to the Territory, the sum of, less percentage and mileage, $64.91
                    James A. Fulton,
                        Sheriff and Collector of Brown Co.

The returns of the Sheriff show that twenty-two persons were illegally assessed, not being residents of the Territory on the 1st of March, the time from which the assessment dated. These persons were charged with a tax of $54.34, which being deducted from the full amount of the tax books for the year leaves a legal tax for the whole of Browne county for the year 1856 of $52.07. As it is before shown that John W. Smith was allowed by Doniphan county court $48 for making the assessment, and James A. Fulton was allowed $7.40 for collecting the same, the total taxes that year failed to pay for assessment and collection, by $3.33; and Browne county was $3.33 poorer after collecting the tax than it was before the assessment.

In August, 1857, the commissioner appointed to contract for building a court house reported that he had contracted with A. Heed to build a house for $500; that the work was done, the building received, and that Heed was entitled to his money. This was the first court house owned by the county. It did not prove a very paying investment, as the county sold it not long after, to Sam'l W. Wade, for $100. On the 19th of October, 1857, this court held its last session, and the reign of the pro-slavery dynasty was forever ended in Browne county. While the free-state men, who, during the whole term of their reign, from March to November, were largely in the majority, firmly believed that the legislature that elected these men was utterly illegal and without any just power to act, they wisely concluded that it was better to quietly submit for the short time that would elapse before the election would be held, than to jeopardize the peace and quiet of the community and retard the material interests of the county by resistance to the powers in authority. Simple justice to these commissioners demands that it should be here stated that the free-state men had no occasion to complain of the conduct of this court, and that they were not governed by partisan feelings in their acts—leading free-state men being repeatedly appointed to positions of honor and trust. Up to this time, (Oct., 1857) but three elections had been held in the county under the territorial laws. The first was on the first day of October, 1855, at which there were FOUR VOTES cast, all being for J. W. Whitfield for Delegate to Congress. This is the first recorded vote in the county and is without doubt the first election ever held within its borders. It is to be hoped that candidates for office were correspondingly scarce or the four poor fellows who were entitled to the rights of suffrage would have been "bored" to death. The next election was on the 6th of October, 1856, for Delegate to Congress and members of the legislature. At this election J. W. Whitfield had 16 votes for Delegate and X. K. Stout, B. O. Driscoll and T. W. Waterson, all, at that time, residents of Doniphan county, received 17 votes for members of legislature. On the 13th of June, 1857, an election was held to select two delegates to attend a Constitutional Convention to be held at Lecompton. At this election, Henry Smith received 36 votes and Cyrus Dolman 44 votes in the district comprising Brown and Nemaha counties.

None of these elections really give any just idea of the number of voters in the county at the times of the elections, as the free-state men of the county, acting in harmony with their party throughout the Territory, steadily refused to vote. The act of the legislature providing for the election of delegates to a Constitutional Convention also provided for the taking of a census. This was done in Browne county by Geo. E. Clayton, Probate Judge, there being then no Sheriff. There is no reason to doubt that it was accomplished with as much accuracy as is usual in such enumerations. He gave the number of voters at 205, but made no return of the whole number of inhabitants. Counting three inhabitants to each voter, which at that time would be a very liberal estimate, as a large number of single men were in the county taking "claims," the whole population of the county could not exceed 615. On the 5th of October, 1857, the territorial election for that year was held, and as the free-state men were at the polls in full force, it is safe to say that a full vote was cast. At this election W. G. Sargent was elected Probate Judge; A. B. Anderson and Jacob Englehart, County Commissioners; Moses P. Proctor, Treasurer; Franklin O. Sawin, Sheriff, by a vote of 136 to 72—the vote by townships being as follows:

	FREE STATE.	PRO-SLAVERY.
Walnut Creek	46	3
Lochnane	10	11
Irving	43	23
Claytonville	37	35

By this vote the control of the county passed into the hands of the free-state men, and the pro-slaveryites were ever after in a hopeless minority.

Browne and Nemaha counties at this time constituted the 4th and 5th Rep. districts and were entitled to one member. E. N. Morrill was elected, receiving 283 votes while E. M. Hubbard, the Democratic candidate received 102 votes.

Turning from a consideration of the political organization of the county, your attention is invited to that of its

EARLY SETTLEMENT.

It is hardly probable that any white man was living in the county at the time of the passage of the Kansas-Nebraska Bill. Near its eastern line, in Doniphan county, an Indian Mission had been in existence for years, at which several white persons resided. One of the overland routes to California, or as it is more familiarly known, the "California Trail," entered the county on its eastern border, nearly midway north and south, and wound along on the divides, avoiding all streams on account of difficulty in crossing; passing on the north of Drummond's Branch, crossing the western part of the present site of Hiawatha, then following the divide between the head waters of the Wolf and Walnut, left the county near the present site of Sabetha. Hundreds of teams and thousands of persons had probably passed over this trail during the five preceding years, on their weary journey to the gold mines of the Pacific Coast. A gentleman who made the trip in 1849, afterwards related that while his party, consisting of thirty men, were camping near the head of Drummond's Branch, he, with two others, started out in search of game, and as they came upon the high prairie in sight of the timber at the northwest and at the south, they discovered a small herd of buffalo, and, after a short chase, succeeded in killing one in the timber nearly east of where Hiawatha now stands. From this description of the point where the buffalo were first discovered, it would seem as though it must have been on or near the present site of Hiawatha; and the wood where it was killed was probably on or near the farm now owned by Dr. Seburn. Nothing of interest can be related of the county prior to its settlement by the whites. While the Indians, doubtless, roamed over its prairies and hunted in the beautiful woods that skirt its streams, there is an utter barrenness of romantic traditions and the conclusion is inevitable that the redskins who hunted deer in Brown county were very common place Indians among whom it would have puzzled Cooper to find a hero, or Longfellow a Hiawatha to woo the lovely Minnehaha. There is a tradition that a battle of some magnitude was fought a mile or two east of our present county seat, near a spring on the farm now owned by W. S. Hall, Esq., and the early settlers report that they found skulls scattered around there and, therefore, they named it "Skull Spring." To determine with any degree of certainty who was the first settler is nearly impossible. A dozen men may have settled at the same time in different sections of the county, unknown to each other. Many of the old settlers who are now living in the county can only tell the month they came; and scores who settled here in the early days became dissatisfied and sought other and fairer fields, while many have, doubtless, travelled that journey from which no weary traveler has ever returned. To give the names of those who are known to have been pioneers in opening this county to settlement and to leave the question of priority open, seems the only true course to pursue. Many came in from Missouri, marked claims, made some slight improvements and returned to their homes to harvest their crops, previously planted there, and to spend the winter. Others, coming from a greater distance, made permanent settlements at once. On the 11th day of May, 1854, Thurston Chase and James Gibbons marked claims on Wolf River, the former taking the farm now owned by Mr. Pittman. They remained on their land two or three weeks, seeing no white man during that time. Mr. Chase broke several acres of prairie, and, returning in August, built a small log house which afterwards burned down. On the 25th of May, C. H. Isely and Peter and Christ Luginbuhl left St. Joseph on foot to explore the section of country lying west of that city. The second day they passed the Indian Mission, near Highland, and at noon stopped to rest and take their dinner on the little stream three miles west of Highland. That evening when a few miles east of Hiawatha they were overtaken by a terrible storm and before they could reach the friendly shelter of the timber, night set in and they were obliged to remain on the prairie, unprotected from the storm during the night, which proved a very dark and rainy one. To make it still more uncomfortable, they discovered, during the night, by the vivid flashes of lightning, a small band of Indians with their ponies, near by them. When morning came, Mr. Isely proposed to continue the journey; but the others, thouroughly disgusted with their first experience in pioneer life, refused to go farther, and the party returned to St. Joseph. In June, 1854, W. C. Foster settled in the eastern part of Nemaha county, passing over Brown county, under the impression that it was Indian Trust lands. A few months later, learning his mistake, he settled where he now lives. On August 2, of that year, E. R. Corncilison took a claim on Walnut Creek and on the 11th of the next March moved upon it with his family. His brother Wallace came at the same time. Thomas Brigham took a claim near Padonia at about the same time, and moved his family into the county the following spring. Henry Gragg settled in Powhattan township that fall, and Isaac Sawin and his son Marcellus settled on the farm now owned by Jacob Hayward and immediately commenced improving it. John Belk and his sons, William and King, took claims near Padonia, in November. James L. Wilson, William and Thomas Duncan, and —— Farmer settled near Robinson that summer or fall. William and James Metis took claims on Poney Creek, in November. Jacob Englehart settled on the farm now owned by B. F. Partch, near Hiawatha, and Benj. Winkles and his sons, Geo. G. and Benj. Jr., settled on Walnut Creek in the autumn of that year. Robert Rhea, who now lives southeast of Sabetha, took a claim in 1854. The winter of 1854—55 was a remarkably mild one, the ground remaining so free from frost that plowing could be done during the entire winter. In 1855, quite a number made homes in the new county. It is impossible to give a full or complete list of the names of all who settled in the county during this year. Among them were Amasa Owen, who marked the first road from Hiawatha to Walnut Creek, a year later; Joseph Dean, Jesse Strange, J. K. Bunn, who was one of the first constables in the county; Henry Woodward, James W. Belts, John G. Spencer, Jesse Duval, Henry Smith, afterwards one of the county commissioners of the county, who brought with him three slaves—a negro woman named Lena, and her two children; J. Peevy, Spencer Bentley, Geo. Roberts, Clifton Gentry, E. W. Short, Loyd Ashby, Thomas Hart, W. P. and W. J. Proctor, Stephen Hughes and family—Mrs. Hughes being the first white woman in Robinson township; A. B. Anderson, Ole Nelson, James Bridgman, Wm. Nash, who died in Dec., 1855; E. Huffman, Rudolph Zimmerman, Christian Zimmerman, John Moser, John Wilhoit, Bradford Sweangen, Sol McCall, T. J. Kenyon, John Sperry, Squire Griffeth, J. A. Alford, Thomas Strange, John & Wm. Vincent, Frank J. Robbins, John Poe, Wm. Purket, John Boggs, who died in May, 1857, and John Schmidt. John S. Tyler, afterwards assessor and county commissioner, settled upon the farm where he now lives. Enoch Painter, Philip Weiss, Isaac Chase, J. J. Weltmer, Jonathan Soden, Isaac Oxier, Wm. Webb, James Smith, James Cameron, James Waterson, T. J. Drummond, John Page, Daniel Miller.

Early in 1855, the settlers on Walnut Creek formed a protective association, chose officers and enacted laws for the government of the new community. Rigid laws were enacted by this association to protect its members in their claims and it has been intimated that these laws were frequently stretched to protect them in holding two or three claims each. The sale of intoxicating liquors to the Indians was strictly prohibited. The first trial for violating this code took place at the house of Jesse Padon—a small log hut which all the settlers prior to 1862 will remember as standing on the banks of the Walnut near Schmidt's saw mill. Complaint had been made that Robert Boyd and Elisha Osborn had been selling whiskey to the Indians. The settlers, sixteen in number, had gathered with the firm determination to enforce their laws at all hazards; but one in the whole settlement was absent and he was too ill to attend. When they were ready to proceed, E. R. Corncilison called their attention to the fact that the accused were not present, and asked that they be sent for. This was very summarily overruled and the trial went on. Witnesses were examined; the testimony was direct and to the point; and after a very brief deliberation a verdict of guilty was rendered and it was decided that the stock of liquors held by these men should be destroyed, and that they should pay a fine of twenty dollars and leave the county at once. Padon was appointed to carry out the sentence and the others all went along to assist in enforcing the law. The house in which Boyd & Osborn kept their liquors stood at the edge of Pilot Grove, about three miles from Padonia. When the squad arrived at the house the accused were called out and informed that they had been tried, convicted and sentenced and that the officers of the law were then and there prepared to enforce the order. They replied that they would cheerfully give up their liquors and pay the fine but begged not to be forced to leave their homes. They also promised faithfully that they would never again be guilty of a like act. After the party had duly considered the matter, and taken a "snifter" all around, they concluded that it was too bad to waste such valuable property, so the parties paid the fine of twenty dollars, promised to sell no more fire-water to the Indians, and were allowed to retain their liquors and remain at their homes. The twenty dollars was equally divided among the posse, each receiving $1.25 for his day's work and all returned to their homes.

On the 10th of September, 1855, Joanna Duncan, daughter of William Duncan, was born. She was probably the first white child born in the county. On the 20th of September John Bunn, son of J. K. Bunn was born.

In October of the same year a son was born to John Morse, under circumstances so peculiar that they deserve a record in these sketches. The preceding March he had moved his family from St. Joseph to a claim on Wolf. Too poor to own a team, he had hired one to bring himself, wife and four little ones to the first home he could ever call his own. In a grove on Wolf Creek, east of Robinson, he set up housekeeping—his total earthly store consisting of one quilt, a skillet, a barrel and a gun. He soon built a rude cabin out of rail-cuts and small poles, making it 10 feet square and covering it with "shakes" rifted from the sturdy oaks. Morse is represented as an inoffensive, kind-hearted man, but far more inclined to rove and hunt than to settle down to the hard toil necessary to make a home in the wilds. While he was away on one of his hunting excursions, his wife was confined. Conscious that the time was fast approaching in which another immortal soul would be ushered into existence, she sent the children to the woods to gather wild grapes, and hastily arranging her rude and scanty couch, was delivered of a healthy, living child. With no friendly hand to render her the slightest assistance, she cared for herself, and when the children returned from the woods she presented them with a little brother and went on with her usual household duties.

In 1856, the troubled, excited state of political affairs prevented any large immigration to the Territory. The border counties were controlled by organized bands of border ruffians, who would suffer no outspoken free-state man to remain in the Territory; to such the very decisive alternative was given—leave or die. The infamous Richardson with his band of cutthroats made occasional raids on the eastern border of the county, keeping the settlers in a constant state of terror. Many an old settler remembers well the long and weary nights spent in the corn fields and woods when he dared not remain under his roof. All had dogs, and the barking of these faithful guardians at night was a signal for the settler to take unceremoniously to the brush, trusting that the scoundrels who were hunting his life would have manliness enough to leave unharmed his wife and dear ones. Fortunately for the good name of Brown county, there were no serious outbreaks within its borders. The honest, sober, industrious citizens of both sides did all in their power to preserve the peace and prevent any violation of the law and the kindliest feelings existed between neighbors who were directly opposed to each other politically.

It has not been possible to get a full list of the settlers of 1856, but among them were E. H. Niles, Sam'l and Frank Myers, Wm. Leper, Chas. Smith, ——— Wheeler, Newton Barnes and his brother, Stephen Pilot, Caleb Magill, Jonathan Scott, W. S. Hill, Simeon Wilkinson, Isaac Perkins, Lewis C. Dunn, John Schmidt, D. McFarland, Wm. Gardner, David Peebles, Wm. McBride, John McGuire, M. C. Willis, C. Goff and ——— Goff, Wm. and James Ross, Dr. Nesbit, John H. Maxwell.

In the summer and fall of 1856 several of the afterwards prominent town sites were located. Carson was laid out by D. McFarland and others. Padonia, Plymouth and Lexington were selected by Gen. J. H. Lane, and his associates. Lane had about forty men with him all well armed with Sharps rifles and revolvers. They also had a small piece of artillery, which they buried on Poney Creek when they left the Territory at a later day. Repeated but unsuccessful efforts were made a few years afterwards to find this cannon and from later developments it seems probable that it was secretly removed by members of the company who had assisted in burying it. At Plymouth rude breastworks were thrown up for protection in case of attack, and at Lexington a small fort of hewn logs was erected. Rumors of advancing forces of border ruffians were in frequent circulation and the settlers as well as Lane and his command were in a constant state of excitement.

Claytonville was laid off in the fall of 1856 by Geo. E. Clayton and others.

John Schmidt that year built a saw mill on the Walnut,

near Padonia, and a substantial dam was erected; but all vestige of mill and dam has long since disappeared. The first school ever taught in the county was in 1856. The school house was a small log cabin, which then stood on farm of John Krey, and the teacher was Samuel C. Shields, Esq., now an honored citizen of Highland. This cabin was built in 1855 and was also used as a church. Religious services were held in it soon after it was built. In 1855, Rev. Mr. Allspaugh, of the M. E. Church, held religious services in the grove near John Belk's house. The settlers came in ox wagons and but three women were present in the congregation. These were without question the first religious services ever held by white men in the county.

In the fall of 1856, a company of U. S. troops were sent into the northwestern part of the county for the pretended purpose of protecting the settlers at the elections. As there was not the slightest reason to anticipate any trouble there and as serious troubles did exist in the border counties, and free-state men were not allowed to vote, it seems certain that the troops were designedly sent here where they could not possibly be of any service, to be out of the way of the obliging Missourians who proposed to do the voting for Kansas. A few miles in advance of the troops was John Brown, his two sons, Redpath and one or two others on their way east by Nebraska City and Iowa. During the day a suspicious looking stranger joined their party and travelled with them a few miles. When they crossed Poney Creek, John Brown, who was suffering from malarial fever, concluded to stop with Morgan Willet, whom he well knew to be as true as steel, and the rest of the party travelled on. After travelling a mile or two, the stranger made some excuse and left the party. Brown's sons were at once suspicious and as soon as night set in went back and got their father and hurried on their journey. About midnight Willett's house was surrounded by troops who demanded that John Brown be given up to them; but the bird had flown and was then safe in Nebraska. Fortunately, too, for some of those soldiers, for the gallant old hero was prepared to sell his life dearly, for he had forty shots, all ready. In the western part of the county, running north and south, was a road much travelled by free-state men and known to all as Jim Lane's road. When it was impossible for a northern man to travel undisturbed through Missouri, hundreds and thousands came into the Territory and left it over this road. Brown knew this road well and often travelled it. He established on it an "under ground railroad" with frequent stations, kept by true and trusted men, who loved liberty better than life and who sympathized most heartily with the poor slaves. The line extended from Lawrence and Topeka to Nebraska City, and thence eastward. Mr. Smith, who lived east of Grenada, kept a station in this county. These stopping places were from 14 to 20 miles apart, depending, of course, upon finding men who could be trusted. Geo. Graham, afterwards senator from this district and State Treasurer, was agent at Albany and did noble service in the good cause. In 1859 they became suspicious of some agents in Nebraska, and to guard against possible failure, sent guides from Albany through to Iowa. W. B. Slosson, now a resident of Sabetha, and John L. Graham, a gallant soldier who afterwards fell while leading his company at the battle of Chicamauga, made several trips in charge of these fugitives. Hundreds of poor fugitives passed over this line were kindly fed and cared for until they had safely passed beyond the reach of the slaveholder's lash. In 1859 John Brown conducted his last train over this road. He had 13 slaves—NO NOT SLAVES THEN, thank God—fugitives with him, and when south of Holton and between that place and Topeka, he was surrounded by a band of border ruffians. Brave old John Ritchie came up from Topeka with 30 men, released him from his danger and escorted him through to Albany. Several of his comrades on that trip were with him afterwards at Harper's Ferry and suffered with their noble leader. In November, 1857,

Brown was detained on Poney Creek by a severe storm and for several days was kindly cared for by Jonathan Scott and family. There is no doubt the staunch free-state element of Brown county had much to do in moulding the sentiments of our State.

Few persons who have not experienced the hardships and deprivations of a settlement in a new country can at all realize what they are. The settlers of 1854 were from forty to fifty miles from any point where they could obtain supplies. The city of St. Joseph was their nearest trading point and to that city they went for their mails also. They had but scanty supplies to start with : for without exception they were poor—rich men are seldom found among pioneers. With but little means to replenish their scanty stock when exhausted, they struggled on enduring hardships and privations utterly unknown to you now. The nearest neighbor often miles away; no physician within a day's ride, they were forced to care for themselves as best they could. One little incident illustrates most strikingly the inconvenience of being so remote from larger settlements. A gentleman and his son, felling trees, one frosty morning in the winter of 1855—56, to fence their farm, had the misfortune to break their axes. Before they could resume their work they were compelled to go to St. Joseph, fifty miles away, with an ox team to get new axes. In 1856 a trading point was built up at Iowa Point and for two or three years supplies for the whole county were purchased there. All old settlers will remember, very kindly, W. D. Beeler, and R. M. and C. M. Williams, who sold thousands of dollars worth of goods to be brought into this county. The spring of 1857 opened with far brighter prospects for the new Territory. Peace was, in a great measure, restored. The free-state element had steadily increased, notwithstanding the determined effort to establish slavery on its soil. The troubles of the preceding two years had advertised Kansas all over the country, and a large immigration was the natural result. At this time there were few houses in the county that could by any stretch of the imagination be called comfortable. There were hardly more than a hundred families in the county, and these occupied small cabins built, almost without exception, near the timber that skirts the streams. Few of these buildings had more than one room. The new comers received a hearty welcome and were most hospitably treated, but the accommodations were but scanty at the best. Early in that spring quite a colony came from Maine, among them W. G. Sargent, Noah Hanson, George Ross, Sumner Shaw, —— Deering, J. G. Leavitt, I. P. Winslow and the writer. On Walnut Creek many of the new settlers found homes with E. H. Niles while they were erecting houses for themselves. His house consisted of two small log cabins about twelve by fourteen feet standing about ten feet apart and connected by a roof. In one of these cabins there was a low attic. Mr. Niles' family consisted of himself, wife and six children, and yet for weeks he had thirteen boarders, making in all twenty one persons who found lodging in that small house. Few of those who enjoyed the hospitality of Mr. and Mrs. Niles will ever forget the many little acts of kindness so acceptable to the stranger in a strange land. Both have since crossed the dark valley.

Another family, noted for its hospitality to those who were seeking homes, was that of John Doe, a noble, generous hearted Kentuckian, who lived near the mouth of Mulberry Creek. His house was built of logs and was about sixteen feet square and contained one room. Yet with a family of seven, during all the spring and summer of 1857 they provided for quite a number of boarders. Padonia House was another famous boarding place. To provide sleeping room bunks had been built against one side of the cabin one above another. One could find representatives of all kinds of society among the new settlers. Men who had occupied leading positions in society in the east and who had met with pecuniary reverses, sought homes in the new territory where they could commence anew surrounded by those equally unfortunate. Lawyers, who had great ideas of their ability to make successful farmers and who in their imaginations had counted their cattle upon a thousand hills, were often found among them. On the other hand could be found the " poor white " of the south with hardly energy enough to hold the plow. It was a strange mixing of all classes and kinds. Almost every state in the Union was represented. Some of these held views that would hardly be acceptable in their native states. For instance, the most bitter anti-slavery man was from South Carolina. The pro-slavery men hunted him down, threatening his life and offering a reward for his head. No language at his command was too bitter for him to use. A favorite expression of his with which he usually closed his tirades was, " D——n them, they'll sup the cup of sorrow with the spoon of repentance before they die!" With thousands and thousands of them this was literally verified before the war closed. The curse returned and rested upon their heads with a vengeance. Our South Carolinian still lives, as loyal as ever to the cause of freedom and rejoices most heartily over the downfall of his enemies. Early in 1857 religious meetings were held, the Methodists having regular service near Robinson. They also organized a church at the house of Wm. Belk on the farm now owned by Peter Pfeiffer. Rev. Mr. Towne, a Baptist clergyman and prominent land speculator, held services at house of E. H. Niles, that spring, which were well attended, but after the Iowa Trust sale the places that had known him knew him no more.

The Iowa Indian Trust lands, lying in Brown county and embracing several thousand acres of her choicest lands, were advertised to be sold to the highest bidder on the 4th of June, by the Secretary of the Interior.

In many cases lands brought more than they could be sold for now. One of the most astonishing features of this excitement was the utter absence of crime, unless gambling could be called a crime, and that was not considered so by these men. There were no thefts—no man was murdered for his money and yet men travelled all over the county, unarmed, with their pockets filled with gold.

While this was going on on the Trust lands, sturdy men who wanted homes for themselves and their families were quietly taking up the Government lands and at the close of the year nearly all the choice lands of the county had been selected. After the sale of the Trust lands on the 4th of June, the most of those who had held these lands left them, the rude shanties were quickly removed and that section of the county was owned largely by wealthy speculators. It would be useless to attempt to enumerate the settlers of 1857. The immigration of that year was probably the largest of any year, though it was by no means permanent. Hundreds left as soon as they had perfected title to their lands without making any real improvements. Two settlers of that year, however, deserve a passing notice—Hon. S. A. Kingman, lected a member of Supreme Court from this county and who is now the honored Chief Justice of the State; and Hon. W. W. Guthrie, who was afterwards elected Attorney General of the State. These men labored earnestly to advance the material interests of the county and for them the people of the county will ever have a warm place in their hearts. That spring many town sites were laid off and many men got immensely rich prospectively selling town lots. Hiawatha, Hamlin, Powhattan, Robinson, Skeenona, Denohu and others were located by men who felt confident that thriving little villages at least could be built up in a short time. At Hamlin, on the farm now owned by A. M. Aldrich, a steam saw mill was erected by Ross & Morrill. This mill burned to the ground on the 3d of April, 1858, rebuilt 2 miles south at junction Walnut & Mulberry creeks.

During that summer regular religious services were held in the woods on E. H. Niles farm and a Sabbath school was organized with David Peebles as Supt. This was without doubt the first Sabbath school in the county. A school house was built at Robinson and the following year David Guard, a hoosier school master, taught in it.

On the 4th of July, 1857, the day was duly celebrated for the first time in the county by a public gathering in the woods on the farm of John Poe on Mulberry Creek. W. C. Foster presided. Dan'l McFarland delivered the oration and N. Hanson read the toasts. W. G. Sargent and others made speeches. Some two or three hundred people were in attendance. The settlers in the summer of 1857 felt sorely the need of some mail facilities and on Walnut Creek they made a contract with Philip Weiss to make a weekly trip to Iowa Point, the nearest post office, 25 miles away, and bring their mail matter. A list of names was furnished him and a request made upon the post master at Iowa Point to deliver letters to him. This was probably the first mail route in the county and was purely a private enterprise. For this service Mr. Weiss received from the settlers $2 for each trip. He combined with it a passenger, freight and express line, doing all with one pair of horses and a lumber wagon. At this time few of the settlers owned horses—nearly all of the farm work, and travelling, even, being done with oxen. Under an act of 1855, a mail route had been established from St. Joseph via Highland to Marysville, Kansas, but service was not put on this route until 1858. August 8, 1857, the first post office was established in the county and George E. Clayton was appointed postmaster. A list of all the post offices that have ever been established in the county, with date and name of postmaster is herewith given.

Claytonville, Aug. 8, 1857,   George E. Clayton.
Mount Roy, Sept. 2, 1857,   Shelton Duff.
Padonia, October 20, 1857.   Orville Root.
Hamlin, December 5, 1857,   Edward H. Niles.

Carson, December 9, 1857,   Marcellus L. Sawin.
Poney Creek, June 21, 1858,   Morgan Willett.
[Discontinued September 19, 1861.]
Robinson, June 20, 1858,   Sam'l W. Wade.
Hiawatha, July 13, 1858,   Hartwin R. Dutton.
Tyler's, March 23, 1864,   John S. Tyler.
Ununda " " "   Giles Chipman.
[Discontinued March 20, 1871.]
Fairview, March 23, 1869.   Orlando Fountain.
Buncomb, May 2, 1870,   Wm. B. Dickinson.
[Name changed to St. Francis Nov. 22, 1871, and discontinued Nov. 11, 1872.]
Grand Prairie, July 27, 1870,   Josiah C. Thomas.
Marak, August 3, 1870.   Franz Marak.
Morrill, December 14, 1870,   Sol. R. Myers.
Mannville, January 9, 1871.   Thomas Mann.
Discord, June 22, 1874,   Benj. M. Hale.

During the summer of 1857 the first house was built in Hiawatha. It was a frame building and stood on the ground now occupied by the Bank. The first occupant of the house was Seth Barnum who kept a hotel in it for several months. A. J. Selleg then occupied it for hotel purposes until the present Hiawatha House was completed in 1859. The first term of the district court was held in the old hotel building in 1858, Judge Petit, now one of the judges of the supreme court of Indiana, being the presiding Judge. The clerk had lost some of the papers, and the Judge, thoroughly disgusted with the court house, refused to try any cases and adjourned the court until the next term. The building has long since been torn down. The second building in Hiawatha is the one now occupied by E. W. Butt Esq., as a residence. It stood upon the lot now occupied by the post office building and was used for a store by H. R. Dutton and B. L. Rider. They sold out in 1858 to W. B. Barnett, the stock of goods invoicing about $75. This was not the first store in the county, however, as M. L. Sawin opened a small store early in 1857 where the Carson school house now stands: The third building in the town was the one now occupied by Mrs. E. J. Chance. This was for some time used for Probate Judge's office and in it he held Probate court. The next season quite a number of buildings were erected. In August, 1857, the free-state men held a convention at Drummond's grove on farm now owned by Col. Bierer to discuss political topics and to decide what course to pursue in the coming elections. The free-state men of the territory, repudiating the bogus pro-slavery legislatures, elected by the people of Missouri had organized a government for themselves under the "Topeka Constitution" and had steadily refused to take part in any territorial election. At this convention, however, the free-state men of Browne county decided to elect officers under the Topeka Constitution in order to be in accord with their party throughout the State and at the same time they claimed it to be the right of every free-state man to vote at the territorial elections in order to wrest the reins of government from the minority party who had so outraged all sense of justice by their conduct. The result was that Ira H. Smith and W. W. Guthrie were elected under the Topeka Constitution and at the ensuing territorial election the free-state men engaged heartily in the canvass with the result before stated.

In September the free-state men held a convention to nominate candidates for the offices to be filled at the territorial election. Though Claytonville was at that time the county seat, the convention was called to meet at Hiawatha. There were but two buildings on the town site and no others within miles of the place. Neither of these buildings were large enough to hold the convention, so they held their session on the open prairie near where the Dispatch office now stands, using a lumber wagon for a speakers' stand. Hon. W. G. Sargent was nominated for Probate Judge, which was the most important office to be filled. Jacob Englehart and A. B. Anderson for commissioners, F. O. Sawin for Sheriff and Moses P. Proctor for Treasurer. As has been before stated, all were elected.

In the early summer of this year, a party on Walnut Creek was tried for theft, and as this was the first trial for a crime of this character, it deserves a passing notice. Two young men, Smith and Elder, from Maine were carrying on the farm owned by Noah Hanson. While they were in the field one day a pistol and a watch were stolen from the cabin. A worthless fellow named Turpin was suspected, and on being arrested, the stolen property was found on his person. He was taken before Esq. Foster for trial; but no copy of the statutes could be found and Mr. Foster very sensibly decided that he could not try the prisoner without "law," and the trial was consequently postponed. The settlers were not satisfied with this tardy administration of justice, so a court was speedily organized at Sawin's store and W. W. Guthrie was chosen Judge. The fellow was tried, convicted and sentenced to pay a fine of five dollars and costs and it was ordered that he stand committed until the fine was paid. But there was no place in which to confine him and it was accordingly arranged that he be allowed to work out the fine and costs at 75 cents per day; and he was turned over to Mr. Smith, to whom the property belonged. Smith put him at work hoeing corn; but during the second day a good opportunity offering he ran away and the fine still remains unpaid.

The asssessment roll of 1857, as returned by Joseph Brown, assessor, is quite a curiosity and shows that on the 1st of March of that year there was the following property in the county:

4 Slaves valued at		$ 1,400
135 Horses & mules valued at		10,903
684 Cattle	" "	15,855
1 Pleasure Carriage	" "	15
54 Time Pieces	" "	390
Money		3,500
Bonds & Notes		2,415

The total taxable property of every description that year amounted to

$38,078, while the whole number of tax payers was 130. At the election held on the 6th of October, 1857. and in which the free-state men participated, three commissioners were to be chosen to locate a permanent county seat. I. P. Winslow, Isaac Chase and I. B. Hoover were elected. Among the many town sites that had been located during the summer there were many contestants for the honor. These commissioners met on the 14th of December, organized their board and took one ballot—the result showing one vote each for Hiawatha, Carson and Padonia. The next day the board visited the town sites of Carson, Hamlin, Padonia and Hiawatha and examined the proposals made by the different companies to donate property or money to the county in consideration of receiving the county seat. Padonia offered to donate a square of ground and a three thousand dollars court house ; Hiawatha offered a building 20 by 30 feet for a court house and every alternate lot on the town site. Carson offered one-half of the lots and fifteen hundred dollars in building material and labor. A second ballot was then taken and resulted as before. A third ballot showed two votes for Carson and one for Padonia. A fourth ballot was unanimous for Carson and the county seat was accordingly removed from Claytonville to Carson. But it was not to remain there long. At the session of the legislature the following January an act was passed authorizing an election to be held April 5 submitting to a vote of the people the question of the location of the county seat. An election was accordingly held and upon the canvass of the vote by the commissioners the returns from four precincts were thrown out on account of irregularity. The vote as canvassed showed that Hiawatha had 128 votes, Carson 37, Hamlin 25, Claytonville 20, Washington 13, Prairie Springs 4 and Padonia 2 ; and Hiawatha was declared the permanent seat of justice of the county and no change has since been made.

On the 10th day of November, 1857, the new commissioners elected by the free-state men, met.

Their first act was to appoint Ira H. Smith county surveyor. This was doubtless done so promptly as a mark of appreciation of his course in refusing to accept any favor or position at the hands of the pro-slavery board. David Peebles was then appointed county clerk in place of Waterson and John S. Tyler assessor in place of Brown. On the 21st of December, the court met again and for the last time at Claytonville, adjourning to Carson to hold their next session on the 28th of the same month. At this session Moses P. Proctor, the Treasurer, tendered his resignation and Sam'l W. Wade was appointed to fill the vacancy; and Henry Rymal was appointed coroner. On the 21st of Dec., 1857, an election was held under the Lecompton constitution for State officers and members of the legislature. No provision was made for a vote squarely against the Lecompton constitution. All votes had to be "For the Constitution, with Slavery." or "For the Constitution, without Slavery." The free-state men, generally, very properly refused to vote either way upon that question; but upon the question of officers under tha constitution, they wisely concluded that it would do then far less harm in the hands of their friends than in those o their enemies. Brown and Nemaha still constituted on Representative District and E. N. Morrill was electe member of the Lower House. On the 4th of January 1858, under the authority of an act of the free-state legisl ture, passed at their session in December, 1857, an ele tion was held allowing a square vote for or against tl Lecompton constitution. In our county 187 votes we cast against it—the pro-slavery men refusing to vote all at this election. On the 11th of January, 1858, t' county commissioners court rose to the dignity of sitti in chairs (they had previously used boxes and benche and ordered the sheriff to procure four arm chairs a eight common ones. This was in those days consider "putting on style." But little business was transacted these sessions except to locate roads and allow accou against the county. At the March term of the co the Sheriff, Fulton, made his final settlement as collector of the county. It is herewith given in full:

BROWNE COUNTY,
   IN ACCT. WITH JAMES A. FULTON.
                              Collector of Revenue.
Cr. By tax book of 1857. $348.22
Dr. By Delinquent list as attached, $285.27
  " Percentage for collecting revenue.   2.95
  " Warrant paid to County Treas.   39.01
  " On hand due Territory including per cent. 20.99
                                             $348.22

Then follows a list of delinquents, embracing many of the prominent men of to-day. The free state men would pay no taxes to pro-slavery authorities, and the pro-slavery men wisely concluded that they would not pay all the tax, so nobody paid. The heaviest tax payer that year was Henry Smith who owned three slaves upon which he was assessed. His tax was $10.95.

On the 12th of April, 1858, the board held its last session at Carson, and on the 19th (a noted day in the history of the United States,) i's first session in Hiawatha was held. On the 24th of May the Commissioners appropriated $2,900 to build a court house with jail and offices attached, and Joseph Klinefelter was appointed special commissioner to let the contract and superintend the building of same. The Legislature, at their session in 1858, passed an act providing that three supervisors should be elected in each municipal township, one of whom should be designated on the ballot as chairman, and the chairmen of the several township boards should constitute the county tribunal. Election to be held on the fourth Monday of March. As this act did not go into effect in time for an election that spring, the old board of commissioners held over, but at their session on the 21st of June the board ordered an election to be held on the 22nd of July in the several townships for the purpose of organizing under the new law.

At this election Samuel A. Kingman was elected chairman of the Board of Supervisors for Irving township, Roger P. Smith for Walnut Creek and James Round for Claytonville. The records do not show that any one was elected in Lochnane township, nor does it appear that that township had any representation on that board.

The old board held a session on the 17th day of July. H. R. Dutton was appointed Commissioner of Public Buildings to fill vacancy occasioned by death of Joseph Klinefelter. On the 16th of August the board again met, but the clerk refused to meet with them or recognize them as a legal body. He was accordingly deposed and C. T. Whittenhall was appointed County Clerk. The records fail to show why the clerk refused to act, nor does it appear that the board transacted any further business or ever met again.

The new board of supervisors met for the first time on the 16th of October, 1858, and organized by electing R. P. Smith chairman and Wm. B. Barnett county clerk. This board was evidently composed of clear headed business men, for one of their first acts was to order the clerk " to report to the court the amount of the appropriations heretofore made by the county board, the amount of warrants drawn, the amount paid on said warrants, and the amount of indebtedness of the county."

This report, made at the next session, showed that warrants had been issued amounting to $4136.65. That appropriations had been made for which no warrants had been issued to the amount of $2960. That all the warrants paid amounted to but $549.58, with nothing in the treasury. It was also found that warrants amounting to $74.90 had been issued and had not been entered on the record. This showed an indebtedness of $4621.97. H. R. Dutton, building commissioner, reported that he had contracted with S. W. Wade to build a court house, and that same was to be completed on or before Aug. 1st

1859. At the election for members of the legislature, in Oct. 1858, Geo. Graham, of Seneca, was chosen to represent Brown and Nemaha counties in the territorial legislature. On the 25th of November E. A. Spooner was appointed Superintendent of Public Instruction, but he declined the office and James A. Stanley was subsequently appointed. In the fall of this year (1858) a grand jury was empannelled for the first time in the new county.

The year 1858 will be remembered by the early settlers as a very wet one. The months of April and July were especially noted for the heavy rainfalls; the streams overflowed their banks rendering it impossible to cross them for days in succession. John Ayres built a steam saw mill at Robinson during that season, and afterwads attached a small run of burrs. There was but little immigration that year. Many who had acquired title to their lands left ; those who remained had raised but little grain the year before, few having farms opened, as all had generally used up the little store they brought with them, they felt most forcibly the effects of hard times. The harvest of 1858 proved a good one, though the wheat was much injured by the rains; but there was little market for anything the farmers had raised, and while breadstuffs were abundant they had no ready money. To add to the distress, President Buchanan, unheeding the earnest appeals for postponement, had ordered a sale of the public lands in this land district, thus compelling preemptors to pay for their lands or run the risk of having their homes sold to merciless speculators. Many of the early settlers bought land warrants worth, then, $140, by giving mortgages on their homes for $250, payable in one year, worth twelve per cent. interest, while others hired money at sixty per cent. to pay for their lands. While the winters of 1855–56 and 1856–57 had been very severe, of one the mercury falling to 30° below zero, the winters of 1857–58 and 1858–59 were noted as very mild ones. In winter of 1856–57 the severe cold weather drove the deer in large numbers to the timber for shelter where they were easily killed. It is said that David Peebles killed seventeen during that season. At the election of township officers in March, 1859, John Belk was chosen chairman of the board of supervisors for Irving township, James Rounds for Claytonville, L. B. Hoover for Walnut Creek and Urias Billman for Lochnane. These gentlemen constituted the county tribunal, and met for the first time on the 30th of May and organized by electing James Rounds chairman and Henry Graves clerk.

In June an election was held for members of the Wyandotte constitutional convention, and Samuel A. Kingman received 93 votes and Samuel Shields 19. The convention met on the 5th of July and organized by electing Samuel A. Kingman temporary president. On the 4th of October the constitution framed at Wyandotte was submitted to a vote of the people, the vote in Brown county being 269 for to 163 against. On the Homestead clause, which was submitted separately, the vote was 173 for to 163 against. On the 6th of Dec. the election for officers under Wyandotte constitution was held and Samuel A. Kingman, of Brown county, was elected Associate Justice of the Supreme Court.

Brown and Atchison counties composed the Second Senatorial District, and elected John A. Martin and H. R. Dutton Senators by a vote of 925 to 574 for Sam'l W. Wade and G. O. Chase. Ira H. Smith represented Brown county in the lower house. H. R. Dutton at the territorial election, held Nov. 8th, had been elected to the House of Representatives of the Territorial legislature.

The autumn of 1859 found the settlers with an abundance of grain though there was little demand for it, and money was extremely difficult for them to get. While they had an abundance of those things that they could produce from the soil by their sturdy labor, it required the closest economy to provide the numberless little necessaries, without which a family can hardly be said to be comfortable these days. Those who had hired money the year before, at ruinous rates to save their homes, found pay-day near at hand without the means to meet the claims against them. In the summer and autumn of 1859 the Pike's Peak excitement was at its hight, and hundreds of teams passed through the county on their way to the gold fields. This made some demand for corn, butter, eggs, milk, &c., and those farmers who happened to be living on the line of the road were very much benefitted by it. As an illustration of the scarcity of money among the settlers at this time, the following incident is related:

A national Republican convention was to be held in the summer of 1860 to nominate candidates for President and Vice-President. The friends of Mr. Seward, in the territory, recognizing his able services in behalf of freedom, determined that a delegation should be sent that would support him. A. C. Wilder, the chairman of the Central Committee and a warm supporter of Mr. Seward, wrote a letter to a friend in Brown county, urging that a delegate be sent to the Territorial convention. A County convention was held, but no one could be found able and willing to go. Those who could spare the time had no horses; those who had horses had no money to pay expenses. After fully discussing the matter, it was gravely proposed that a contribution be taken up to defray the expenses of the delegate. This was actually done, some giving twenty five cents, some a dime, others less, until four dollars and fifty cents in legal tender was raised. It was calculated that by close economy this amount would defray the expenses absolutely necessary. Armed with the necessary credentials and a letter to Mr. Wilder commending the gentleman from Brown county to his hospitality, the delegate attended the convention. It was reported at the time that the closing paragraph of the letter informed Mr. Wilder that " Dr. takes his whisky straight." It is needless to add that the delegate has since been twice honored by an election as County Treasurer, and that the author of the letter has since filled most creditably a state office.

In the spring of 1860 there was quite a demand for corn to transport to the new gold mines, and several trains of teams wers loaded in the county. Nearly all who had corn sold the last bushel that they felt they could possibly spare, the need for money was so great, trusting to the genial clime and fertile soil to provide them an abundant harvest. The price of corn at that time, May and June, 1860, was 25 cents per bushel. The winter of 1859-60 had been remarkably dry and not very cold. March and April were windy and without rainfall. Still trusting in Him who has promised seed time and harvest, the people sowed and planted a larger amount than ever before. May and June passed away with scarcely a shower. There was no harvest of small grain for it had utterly failed to mature, and there were very few fields that were cut at all, while there was not one that would pay for the expense of harvesting. The crop of small grain was estimated to average two bushels per acre; but those fields that were not harvested were not included in this estimate. Had they been the real average would not have been half a bushel to the acre. Still the farmers worked away hoping and praying that rain would come in time to save their corn, but they were doomed to bitter disappointment. July and August were absolutely without rain, and not till the cool weather of fall did the long desired showers come—too late for the crops of that year. It was literally a year without rain and an absolute and complete failure of crops of all kinds. Words are inadequate to describe the bitter disppointment of those noble men and women who had struggled through the weary years to make homes for themselves and dear ones, when they found winter approaching and nothing in store for the long and bitter months. Starvation stared them in the face. Surely, it was no fault of theirs. They had toiled unceasingly. They had ploughed and planted. Most faithfully had they watched their young crops, but God had not watered them, and all their labor came to naught. The winter of 1860-61 will never be forgotten by those who spent it in Kansas. But few families in the county lived comfortably while the most had barely the necesssaries of life, and those they had to obtain from day to day as best they could. Fortunately, warm hearts and willing hands were busy in the more favored states gathering for those in need, and many were thus saved from starvation. The most striking feature of that winter was the hearty good feeling that existed between the settlers. To live through the winter and until another harvest time was the most that any hoped to accomplish, and the feeling of dependence that rested upon all, filled them with a hearty sympathy for their less fortunate neighbors rarely manifested in more favored seasons. All were ready to divide their own scanty store with those who had none; and with all the privations and hardships there was a hearty, cheerful, hopeful, manly feeling that spoke volumes in praise of the pioneers. Many passed the whole winter without having groceries of any kind in their houses. Few had a full supply of meat, and potatoes were almost unknown, and many families had little else but corn meal or flour. Many were without sufficient clothing to protect them from the bitter winds of winter, and coarse sacks and old cloth were made to take the place of boots and shoes. But these trials were not without their compensation. Men and women who bore them patiently were made stronger and better by the sufferings they endured, and the Kansas of to-day is stronger, purer and nobler for having suffered in its early settlement. Too much praise cannot be given to the generous hearts in the East who contributed so liberally to the needy. Without their aid thousands would have been compelled to abandon their homes, and hundreds would have starved.

Among the many incidents in the early history of the county, one, occurring in the fall of 1865, deserves special mention. It was called " stealing a grist mill,' and created no little comment at the time. No full statement or explanation of the circumstances has ever before been published. In the early part of 1865, A. M. Hamby, who was running a saw mill at Falls City, induced W. C. Foster, Esq., of this county, to enter into partnership with him. Mr. Foster had a portable grist mill consisting of a run of burrs, the frame supporting them and the necesssary shafting and cog-wheels to run it, which he removed to Falls City and attached to Hamby's saw-mill. Before the partnership was fully consummated and the papers signed, Mr. Foster, becoming convinced that Mr. Hamby's representations were false and that he was very much involved, declined to carry out the arrangement. When he attempted to remove his grist mill Hamby refused to allow him to take it. To engage in litigation in another state in the unsettled condition of affairs, and with the strong feeling in the community in favor of retaining the mill, seemed useless. To abandon altogether the idea of recovering his property was not to be thought of. After consulting with his attorney, he arranged with seven of his friends to go with him and quietly remove the property. The party gathered at his house one pleasant autumn evening with two heavy lumber wagons and four good horses, and when the shades of evening gathered around they started for Falls City. At a little after eleven, reaching the wide bottom lying south of that place, they left their teams in the tall grass in charge of one of their number, and proceeded to make an examination of the premises. In a house near by a light was burning. Silently they moved around among the logs in the mill-yard carefully looking over the situation to decide how to act. The frame of the mill was bolted firmly to the sills of the building. A heavy wrench had been brought along, and as the nut turned on the rusty bolt the creaking iron sounded like filing a saw and caused all to start with the fear that they would be discovered. Industriously they worked and in a few minutes it was carefully lifted from its resting place and laid upon the saw-dust. A span of horses were soon brought up, and hitching to the mill, it was dragged over the soft ground a quarter of a mile or more to where the wagons had been left. In a few minutes it was carefully taken apart and placed in the wagons, and the party were as anxious to get out of Nebraska as they were a few hours before to get in. Quietly they pursued their journey until just as the day was dawning, they came in sight of the timber near Mr. Foster's home. Then the five good singers who were in the party struck up with one accord, "Home, Sweet Home," and never was it sung with a more hearty good will. A few days after, the grist mill was attached to E. N. Morrill,s saw-mill where it did good service for several years. No attempt was ever made to return it to Falls City, all parties, it is presumed, feeling that under the circumstances, the stealing of the grist mill was perfectly justifiable. The spring of 1861 was a very favorable one, and all went to work with a hearty good will to put in the seed again. Thousands of bushels of choice wheat and corn had been donated by the more favored farmers of other states, and thus all were enabled to secure the needed seed. Early in the year, however, the war clouds began to gather and all were watching anxiously the course of events. Largely dependent on Missouri for supplies as the people of Kansas at that time were, uncertain how the people of that state would act in the approaching trouble, the settlers looked anxiously forward to the harvest that would to some extent render them independent of their unfriendly neighbors. The harvest richly rewarded them for their labor, and a more hopeful feeling pervaded the whole community. During the summer companies of home guards were organized in different sections of the county, holding themselves in readiness to protect the lives and property of the citizens. At Hiawatha there was a very large and finely drilled company under command of Capt. I. J. Lacock, and at Hamlin, Capt. L. B. Hoover had command of a good company of true men. At Robinson a company was organized and in readiness, and possibly at other points in the county. In the latter part of summer and early part of autumn, the work of making the crops being over, a large number of the young men went into the service followed during the winter and spring by many others, until few able-bodied men were left behind. The records fail utterly to give to Brown county the credit of her full quota that volunteered in defense of their country. Many were credited to the counties where they enlisted, and others were put down without giving the place of residence. In justice to the brave boys and to the noble county they represented, a list is here given of those who were actual residents of Brown county at the time of entering the army. Many names are, doubtless, omitted that should be here, but the list has been compiled with great care after exhausting all means of information at our command. This list comprises nearly two hundred names. At this time the largest vote that had ever been polled in the county was four-hundred-and-twenty-five, so it would seem that nearly one-half of all the voters in the county went into the army. The following are the names:

A. B. Anderson	Alex. Abshear	John Abshear	J. H. Armstrong
Andrew Armstrong	Simeon Austy	Levi C. Anderson	L. G. Bollinger
Geo. W. Bunce	Chas. T. Boomer	John Barnum	Geo Bird
J. M. Bradford	Geo. H. Burgh	Richard M. Bean	John Brady
John Bertwell	W. H. Bertwell	Eli F. Benton	Robert Bradley
Samuel W. Buckley	T. F. Barnum	J. L. Bradford	C. Beatley
Ashley Chase	Albert Chandler	Melvin Chandler	Chas. Chandler
Frank Chandler	John Y. Cook	Thurston Chase	J. C. Carnes
Thaddeus Corbou	Chas. Cowley	T. B. Cummings	John Croit
Henry Cheal	James Clark	C. M. G. Ousendschou	S. P. Dickinson
H. L. Dean	Sam'l Donaldson	Daniel Ellis	B. S. Eye
A. Ezline	Conrad Englehart	A. C. Foster	h. S. Foster
D. E. Fowler	John A. Furuish	W. H. Furuish	John Foitchter
Martin Ford	R. H. Fletcher	Henry H. Graham	Robert Gaston
Wm. Graham	John L. Graham	Wm. Gentry	Henry J. Gillespie
Joseph S. Hill	B. F. Heartou	Hiram Horton	Henry Hickman
Chas. B. Hauber	John Hauber	Peter Hatheid	W. M. Johnson
Alex. Johnson	James Jellison	Frank D. Jellison	Robert Jemson
Chester Jones	J. K. Klinefelter	S. K. Klinefelter	P. K. Klinefelter
Samuel Kaiserman	Thos. Kelley	Henry Leuen	Daniel Leuen
H. H. Lynn	Peter Lynch	Wm. Linquist	Lewis Lawrencee
D. C. Muire	E. N. Morrill	W. P. Mevinney	Zach. Mallows
Levi Morrill	O. H. McCauley	J. S. Marshall	Abram Marshall
Fraus Marak, Jr.	James J. Miller	Andrew McLaughlin	C. Meisenheimer
S. T. Meredith	Jacob Miller	Thomas Martin	Wm. G. Meredith
A. Meisenheimer	Harvey Nichols	Abram Norwood	A. J. Owen
Daniel W. Owen	David Oldfield	John Oldfield	Geo. S. Osman
E. N. Ordway	S. U. Prolaser	John W. Proctor	Robert Pollock
Joseph H. Poe	P. G. Parker	Jonathan Quick	M. A. Quigley
Stephen Quaile	L. M. Risley	Wm. Richardson	Wm. Richards
A. Richardson	Chas. E. Robinson	Sam'l Richards	John T. Reeves
Marshall P. Rush	John W. Smith	Josiah A. Snively	Albert G. Speer
I. N. Speer	F. M. Stumbo	Adam Schmidt	Michael Schmidt
Isaac A. Sawin	Luther Sperry	J. S. Stillwell	W. G. Sargent
Moses Seveir	Edwin Selleg	B. F. Sweetland	John M. Snively
James F. Starnes	Jacob Sigafous	Jonathan W. Scott	Chas. D. Stumbo
Francis M. Starnes	James Sherman	Isaac Sweetland	John F. Snields
Isaac Selleg	Dudley Sawyer	Wm. Starus	Gottleib Spabe
Newton Seveir	Isaac Schmidt	Benj. F. Strange	John F. Spenser
Eli Swordterger	Jacob Stilwell	Winslow W. Smith	John Smith
David C. Swayzie	F. W. Steigler	Abraham Sumpter	Hesekiah Smith
C. E. Simmonds	Alonzo Scott	Henry Smith	L. H. Slagle
John Sebilling	Francis Sevier	Thos. Strange	Wm. Schmidt
Samuel Teas	Andrew Twidwell	John Uhuan	E. M. Vaughn
Lewis Vaughn	Albert Vaughn	Wm. C. Vassar	Benj. Winkles
J. A. Wilson	Amasiah Wescott	A. D. Westerfield	Henry Wilkins
John Weiss	Phillip Weiss	Sam'l F. Withnow	C. V. Wicks
W. S. Woodcock	Wm. Wilkinson	A. H. Watson	W. C. Wyatt
	Edward Hickman	John Zimmerman	

Brown county has its list of martyrs who sacrificed their lives to save their country. Henry H. Graham, John L. Graham, John W. Smith, Josiah A. Snively, Daniel Lanch, L. C. Bolinger, Samuel Donaldson, D. U. Muire, E. M. Vaughn, Edwin Seely, James Sherman, John Y. Cook,

Samuel Keiserman, W. S. Woodcock, Abraham Sumpter, J. A. Wilson, L. M. Risley, T. B. Cummings, Chas. B. Hauber, Simeon Ansty, J. L. Bradford, John Hauber, Newton Leveir, John N. Spaurer and Samuel F. Withrow all sleep the "sleep that knows no waking" in southern grsves; but their brave comrades who survive will ever cherish their memories, and the true and the good will ever hold in grateful remembrance the names of our fallen heroes.

The Legislature of 1860 again changed the law in relation to county courts, and adopted the old plan of electing three commissioners to transact county business. At the election, held Nov. 26th, 1860, W. B. Barnett, Isaac B. Hoover and James Rounds were elected county commissioners, and met on the 2nd of April, organizing by choosing W. B. Barnett chairman. Henry Graves had previously resigned as county clerk, and H. R. Dutton had been appointed. One of the first acts of this board was to require the clerk to make out a statement of the receipts and expenditures of the county from the time of its organization to April 1st, 1860. This report shows that the total amount

of warrants issued was	$7,713.02
Amount of appropriations for which no warrants had been issued	835.00
Total amt. of appropriations	$8,548.02
The total amount of warrants redeemed	$2,187.18
Taxes due on lands bid in by county	300.90
Tax due on roll of 1859	4231.01
Total	$6718.09

Leaving an indebtedness of $1828.93

The tax levy for this year was five mills on the dollar. On the 4th of April David Peebles was appointed Superintendent of Schools in place of James A. Stanley, resigned. The reasons for Mr. Stanley's resignation are not given, but as the records of the county show that the commisioners allowed him $8.00 for the first six months services, it is not strange that he did not desire to continue in the office. The new Superintendent, however, did better, as he received $12.00 for his first three months services. This board of commissioners only held their positions until the regular election in November, of 1860, when James Round, Lewis C. Dunn and Wm. Vassar were elected. James Round was chairman of this board. Mr. Vassar, however, went into the army early in the autumn of 1861, and Thos. Ellis was appointed to fill the vacancy.

In the spring of 1861 the first paper ever printed in the county was struck off; Dr. P. G. Parker was editor and proprietor, and the sheet was called the Brown County Union. Its publication was continued through the summer and autumn, but in the winter the office was entirely destroyed by fire and no effort was made to continue its publication. The office was in the lower story of the building owned by H. M. Robinson, Esq., and stood on the ground now occupied by the law office of Killey & May. Mr. Robinson was at the time living in the upper story of the building, and narrowly escaped with himself and family, losing all of their household goods.

In March, 1861, H. R. Dutton, Senator from this district, was appointed State Treasurer to fill a vacancy, and at the following election he was elected to that office. W. B. Barnett was elected Senator to fill this vacancy. At the general election, in Nov., 1862, W. W. Guthrie was elected Attorney General of the state, being the third state officer taken from Brown county. Since the expiration of his term of office, this county has had no representation on the state board, though it is believed that there have been residents of the county who would have accepted positions had they been elected.

At the election, held Nov., 1861, James Round, Thos. Ellis and Noah Hanson were elected commissioners, and E. L. Pound county clerk. Thos. Ellis was elected chairman. The term of office of this board commenced Jan.

1st, 1862 and ended Jan. 1st, 1864. The records, during the time, show nothing of special interest, except that the board observed the most rigid economy in their appropriations, and by liberal levy did much to improve the credit of the county. Their levy for 1862 was five mills, and for 1863 seven mills.

In December of 1863, James Round, who had served the county faithfully as a commissioner for several terms, met his death by the accidental discharge of a gun in his own hands. At the session of the board, held Jan. 4th, I. P. Winslow was chosen to fill the vacancy. At the same session the board appropriated $3,000 to build a jail, and appointed W. B. Barnett commissioner to take charge of the work. This was the last session of this board. On the 4th of April, 1864. M. C. Willis, I. P. Winslow and Isaiah Travis, who had been elected at the Nov. election, assumed the duties of the office. E. A. Spooner had been at the same time elected clerk. This board organized by choosing M. C. Willis chairman. Upon consideration of the jail question, they decided that they had no authority to erect public buildings without first submitting the question to a vote of the electors of the county, and they therefore discharged the commissioner from further duty in the matter. At their session in the following July, they decided to submit the question of building a jail to a vote of the people at the next general election. The records of the county fail to show that any vote was taken upon this subject, but it seems that a vote was taken to decide whether the school lands in the county should be sold or not, and it was decided in the affirmative by a vote of 208 to 65. A most unfortunate decision for the school fund, as five years later the lands were worth three times as much At the Jan. session, 1865, Mr. Travis tendered his resignation as county commissioner, and William Morris was appointed to fill the vacancy. On the 22nd of Oct., 1865, E. L. Pound, County Treasurer, died, and at a special term of the court, held for that purpose, the following resolutions were passed:

"WHEREAS, in the mysterious ordering of Divine Providence, E. L. Pound, Treasurer of Brown county, has been removed by sudden disease and death, therefore

Resolved, that it is fitting that we should place upon record at this time, being called upon to appoint a successor to fill the vacancy caused by this death, our appreciation of his uniform kindness in all our official intercourse. His fidelity to the interests and responsibilities entrusted to his care and perfect integrity in the discharge of the duties of his office, have won for him our highest esteem and affectionate regard. And while we mourn his departure as the loss of a dear, worthy and beloved friend, we feelingly tender our sympathies to the family of the deceased, who are thus suddenly overwhelmed with grief in the loss of a kind, affectionate and beloved husband and father."

W. B. Barnett was appointed treasurer to fill the vacancy.

At the election in November, a vote was taken on the jail question, resulting in a vote of 198 for building a jail to 96 against. Subsequently, however, objections were raised that the vote was not a fair one, as only printed ballots in favor of the proposition were furnished at the polls, and a new election was ordered and the proposition was defeated. This seems to have been a wise decision on the part of the voters, for the county has been so comparatively free from crime that it has cost much less to keep the prisoners in the jail of the adjoining county than to maintain a prison at home. The records of the county show that in twenty-one years, from the first settlement of the county in 1855 to July 1876, there have been but thirty-three convictions for crime of all classes. Of these eight were for assault and battery. Thirteen were for grand larceny, the offense being, with few exceptions, horse stealing, and in almost every case committed by non-residents of the county while passing through it. The other twelve convictions were divided as follows: Petty larceny, 3; perjury, 1; forgery, 2; gaming, 2; selling liquor, 4. The total length of all the sentences was forty-three years and the total fines $675. It is questionable whether any other county in the United States can present a more favorable showing in this respect. Brown county to-day has no jail. Who will say that one is needed?

This board of commissioners managed the finances of the county with great care and prudence. Early in their term of office, July, 1864, county warrants were at par, and from that time to the present, a period of twelve years, no county warrant has ever been presented at the treasurer's office that was not promptly paid at its par value.

But little of general interest or importance occurred in the county during the war. Those who remained at home cultivated their farms, and as the seasons were favorable and prices high all improved their condition pecuniarily. So many, however, were absent in the army that many fields were left untilled, and at the close of the war there were hardly as many acres under cultivation as at the commencement. While there had been a considerable increase in wealth, there had been no immigration and consequently no increase in population. In 1865 there was a very general return of the soldiers, and to their praise, let it be said, they engaged heartily in active work and were the same steady, true, industrious men that they were four years before, when the excitements and temptations of army life were unknown to them. At the close of the war real estate in the county was extremely low. There was indeed no demand at all for it, and choice tracts of land could be bought, within a few miles of Hiawatha, at three dollars per acre. A choice tract of land, 120 acres, near Morrill station, was sold during the war for a hundred dollar bill, and this when gold was at a hundred per cent. premium. In 1866 there was a slight immigration to the county, and this steadily increased during 1867, 1868 and reaching its height in 1869. The increase in the three years being nearly two hundred per cent. New farms were opened and improvements of all kinds were rapidly carried forward. The county after all its hardships and deprivations had awakened to a new life. Among the causes producing this increased activity, no one was more prominent or did more to attract the attention of the people of other states than the liberal advertising of the Central Branch Union Pacific R. R. Co.

KICKAPOO RESERVATION.

This company became the possessors of the Kickapoo Reservation under a treaty made with this tribe of Indians, dated June 28th, 1862, and ratified by President Lincoln May 28th, 1863, the Indians reserving only thirty sections near the southwest corner of Brown county, and a few small and scattered tracts were taken by members of the tribe. The company acquired title to 127,832 acres, of which much the larger part was in Brown county. For this large tract of lands the Indians received $1.25 per acre. In 1866 the railroad company advertised these lands for sale, scattering maps and descriptive circulars broadcast over the whole country. The first sale of land made by the railroad company in Brown county, was effected on the 13th of April, 1867. David J. Par.s was the purchaser and the tract is described as lots 6 and 7 of Sec. 2_, Town 3, Range 17. During the year 1867, 13,207 acres were sold, and as the company required all time purchasers to improve one-tenth of their land each year for three years, the Reserve was soon dotted over with farms. Only 18,000 acres of this large tract remains unsold, and more than 1,200 individuals are numbered among the original purchasers. A considerable amount of it has since changed hands and some tracts several times. The land department of the company, during the whole time from its organization until to-day, has been under the direction and complete control of Maj. W. F. Downs, and has been managed with great care and skill. While the interests of the railroad company have been carefully watched and guarded everything has been done that could be consistently to favor the settlers. The utmost leniency has been shown those who were delinquent in their payments, and all have been encouraged in their efforts to make homes. With few, very few exceptions, the purchasers deserved these favors, for few new counties are ever blessed with a more sterling, honest and industrious class of settlers than those who improved the Kickapoo Reserve; and no portion of Brown county can show finer farms or better improvements.

In the north-eastern portion of the county there is still an Indian Reservation belonging to the Iowas, and embracing some 12,000 acres of the choicest lands in the county. The settlement of these lands would add largely to the wealth and population of the county.

THE GRASSHOPPER.

No sketch of the county would be complete that omitted to mention the ravages of this pest, and a very serious question in the minds of thoughtful men, is, whether the visits of the locust are going to be frequent enough in the future to be a serious drawback on farming. It would seem a safe rule to judge the future by the past. Up to 1866 there had been no grasshoppers seen in the county, nor had any resident of the county the slightest reason to apprehend any damage from them. The county had then been settled twelve years, and our people were in blissful ignorance of the existence of this plague. In the latter part of August of that year, reports were brought in by settlers on the frontier that they had appeared there in immense numbers and were very destructive. Day by day reports came that they were drawing nearer, and about the 8th of September they reached the western line of the county, moving from three to twelve miles per day. On the 10th of Sept. the immense army, which no man could number, reached Hiawatha, devouring every green thing from the face of the earth. The corn fields were literally stripped, leaving the bare stalk with the ears hanging to it, and the latter often badly eaten. The corn was too far advanced, however, for them to injure it very seriously, and the only real loss from them that fall was in the destruction of forage. They deposited immense quantities of eggs which hatched out in the latter part of April and early in May. This young crop were, of course, obliged to feed upon whatever was within their reach until they were large enough to travel, and whenever they hatched in large numbers near fields of small grain there was no possibility of raising it. The beaten paths and roads and the newly broken prairie seemed to be favorite locations for depositing their eggs. Many fields of small grain were entirely destroyed that spring, while many others escaped unharmed. The corn was not so much injured though in some localities the early corn was destroyed. About the 29th of June they left and were not again seen during the season. But a small portion of the county was under cultivation then and the total loss was small compared with that of 1874. In the fall of 1868 they again appeared, but far less numerous and causing far less loss. Their appearance at this time caused very little excitement and but slight importance was attached to it; a few eggs were deposited and the following spring a few gardens were injured, but not much attention was paid to it. In the early part of August, 1874, they again appeared. At this time the country west was much better settled, and the railroads, penetrating to the Rocky Mountains, brought the news of the approaching hosts while they were hundreds of miles away and weeks before they reached here. The season had been a very dry one, with frequent, hot south winds, so common an attendant of drouths, and so exceedingly disagreeable. The corn at best would have been nearly a failure, but what little there was of grain or foliage speedily disappeared. Trees were stripped of their leaves. Apple and peach orchards could frequently be seen loaded with rich fruit but without a leaf to protect it from the hot sun. In many cases the fruit was much injured, and it was a common sight to see peach trees hanging full of pits, the meat of the fruit having been neatly nibbled off. In some cases the bark was eaten from trees. Nothing escaped, for they seemed quite indifferent as to the quality of their food. Tomato plants, onions, and even tobacco plants were utterly destroyed. Again they laid their eggs in immense numbers, the ground being literally perforated by them. Heavy freight trains on the railroads were frequently delayed for hours by their gathering on the track in large numbers, the wheels crushing them and forming an oily, soapy substance. The next spring but little apprehension of much damage was felt, and the farmers put in an unusual amount of small grain. When the warm days of spring came the little pests hatched out in numbers far exceeding anything before experienced. The season was unusually favorable for small grain, and on the 1st of May there was as fine a prospect of an abundant harvest as was ever known. Ten days later the myriads of little locusts, fast developing, were rapidly sweeping it away, and on the 1st of June but few fields of grain were left in the county. The eastern part of the county suffered much more than the western half, owing to there having been fewer eggs deposited in the latter section. The corn was much injured; nearly all the first planting was utterly destroyed. Many re-planted at once without waiting until they had passed away, and again lost it all. In one case, a farmer planted two hundred acres four times. Those were indeed, dark days for the farmers. All hope for raising anything for the season was well-nigh gone. The middle of June came and still the locusts tarried. The farmers with wonderful courage and patience had ploughed up their small grain fields where the crop had been destroyed, and were busily engaged in planting corn. From the 12th to the 20th of June an immense amount of corn was planted. In an ordinary season this would have been too late to make any crop, but the season proved most favorable. Rains were frequent and not too heavy. About the 20th of June the grasshoppers commenced leaving, and by the 25th not one could be found. If ever men showed true pluck under discouraging circumstances, the farmers did during the spring of 1875. Braver men never lived—truer men never bit bread. The season continued favorable and an immense crop of corn and vegetables was raised.

RAILROADS.

Early in 1860 an effort was made to build a railroad from St. Joseph, west, through the northern tier of counties in Kansas, and four miles of track was laid connecting Ellwood and Wathena; but the war stopped all work on it, and nothing further was done for several years. In 1866 an attempt was again made to revive the work, and the Legislature of that year donated 125,000 acres of land to the Northern Kansas R. R. Co., an organization that had been formed for the purpose of receiving and making available this donation from the state.

The incorporators of this company met for the purpose of organization at Hiawatha, May 12th, 1866, and elected Thos. Osborn. Geo. Graham, Sam'l Lappin, J. E. Smith, Sam'l Speer, W. B. Barnett, J. D, Brumbaugh, E. C. Manning, D. E. Ballard, F. H. Drenning and E. N. Morrill, directors. Sam'l Lappin was chosen President, F. H. Drenning Secretary, W. B. Barnett Treasurer and D. E. Ballard Land Agent. On the 15th of May a proposition was submitted to the people to issue $125,000 of the bonds of the county to this company to aid in building a railroad through the county, and it was defeated by a small majority. On the 16th of June a vote was again taken upon a proposition to issue $100,000 of the bonds of the county for the same purpose, some of the objectional features of the previous proposition being changed, and it carried by a majority of 102 votes. Soon after, the Northern Kansas R. R. Co. consolidated with the St. Jo. & D. C. R. R. Co., the new organization assuming the latter name. In 1869 the road was graded as far as Hiawatha, and in January, 1870, the first rail was laid in the county. About the 20th of February regular trains commenced running to Robinson, H. M. Robinson taking charge of the station at that place. On the 7th of March

the trains ran to Barnum's field, adjoining the town site of
Hiawatha. A temporary platform was built there, and for
two or three weeks the trains left that point. The present
depot was soon after erected, and as soon as the track
could be laid trains were run to it, the first train reaching
the present Hiawatha depot early in April. H. M. Robinson was placed in charge of the station, and has continued
to discharge the duties ever since to the full satisfaction of
all. From him the following statements of the business of
the road for the months of August, 1870 and 1876, were
obtained:

Freight Received, August, 1870	666,463 lbs
" Forwarded " "	436,299 "
Total	1,102,762 lbs
Freight Received, August, 1876	2,537,973 lbs
" Forwarded " "	2,774,373 "
Total	5,312,346 lbs
Receipts for August, 1870	$1745.34
" " " "	6434.71

With the completion of the road to Hiawatha the town
commenced a rapid growth, which, notwithstanding the
hard times, has continued to a great degree ever since.
The work on the road was pushed rapidly during the
summer of 1870, and in August the cars were running to
Sabetha, in Nemaha county.

SCHOOLS.

The citizens of Brown county, from its early settlement,
have taken an active interest in schools, and the result is
shown in the numerous comfortable and tasty school
houses that are found in every part of the county. Schools
were taught in the county as early as 1856 and 1857, but
the first regular organized district was the "Carson District," organized by Supt. J. A. Stanley. March 11th, 1859.

On the 21st of April the first school board was elected:
Noah Hanson, Director. I. B. Hoover, Clerk
A. M. Kendall, Treasurer.

The next organized district was the one adjoining, in the Myers neighborhood. The Annual Report of the county Superintendent for 1859 shows that there were in Brown county, at that time, 204 children of school age. That two schools had been taught, and that 95 children had attended these schools. The total amount of money raised that year for building school houses was $980. There were four organized districts in the county and two school houses. Now, there are sixty seven school districts wholly within the county, and seven joint districts made up partly of territory within the county. These districts all have houses, and, with the exception of eight or ten, the buildings are highly creditable to the citizens. The total valuation of these buildings including furniture, is $87,000. All of the districts have maintained schools the past year,—none less than three months while many have had nine months; the average in the whole county being more than six months. The total number of children of school age in the county in 1875 was 3332, and the sum of $29,246 was raised for school purposes that year.

CHURCHES.

A brief summary of the different church organizations is all that can be given. In 1857 clergymen of different denominations held regular services throughout the county As there were no church buildings or school houses these meetings were held during the winter, in private houses, and in the pleasant weather of summer in groves. The Methodist, Congregationalist and Baptist organizations were first represented. For the first five years the Methodists had but little strength and gained very slowly. In June, 1861, they had a membership of but fifteen. Revs. Allspaugh, Lawrence, Green and Buffington were the first workers in the new field. In 1861–62 Rev. Mr. Buffington preached on a circuit embracing Sabetha, Padonia, Poney Creek, Hamlin, Capioma and Grenada. On the 12th of April, 1862, a conference was held at Hamlin. At this session E. N, Knapp and John Belk were elected stewards. There were at this time nineteen members in full communion and fifty-eight on probation. The growth of the church was from this time quite rapid. In 1866 they erected their first church building, the substantial stone now standing in Hiawatha. The corner stone was laid with imposing ceremony on the 5th of July of that year. The membership now numbers between three and four hundred, and they have another substantial church edifice at Robinson.

The Congregationalists first organized at house of E. H. Niles, on Walnut creek, Sept. 26th, 1858. Revs. J. H. Byrd and R. D. Parker conducting the services, and eight persons were received into the new church. June 30th, 1859 Rev. G. G. Rice commenced his ministerial labors with this church and continued with them several years. Church organizations are now maintained at Hiawatha, Fairview and Hamlin. This denomination has substantial church buildings at Hiawatha and Hamlin, and a membership in the county of one hundred and twenty.

The Baptists first commenced their work in this county in 1858, the Rev. Mr. Frink being the first regular minister of that denomination. The year before Rev. Mr. Towne had preached several times at house of E. H. Niles, but he left the country immediately after the Iowa Trust Land sales. Rev. Mr. Frink was an able and earnest man, but his labors in the state were short as he died in 1860. In 1859 Elder Hodge, of Michigan, father of Mrs. E. A. Spooner, preached very acceptably on Walnut creek. The first church organization in the county of this denomination was entered into at house of Luther Sperry, near Hiawatha, in 1860. Elder Tibbets, of New York, was moderator of the presbytery that organized this church. It was called the First Baptist church of Hiawatha, and Rev. Mr. Alward preached the sermon on the occasion. This denomination has been represented by able, earnest men and has increased rapidly in the county. It now has in the county, one church building, five organized churches, seven ministers and a membership of nearly four hundred.

The first Presbyterian church in the county was organized by Rev. F. E. Sheldon, at Hiawatha, on the 10th of July, 1870. In July, 1872, Rev. S. T. Davis took charge of the work, and under his earnest and efficient labors the church increased rapidly in numbers. They now have a neat and tasty brick church thirty by forty feet and a membership of nearly fifty. A few months since Rev. Mr.

Davis left for a wider field of labor to the irreparable loss of this church.

The first Christian church in the county was organized by Rev. T. K. Hansberry, in 1868, and was known as the Hamlin and Padonia church, and for three years Mr. Hansberry had charge of it. Now, there are two large churches at these places under the charge of Revs. J. F. Berry and Jas. McGuire. At Hamlin a large church building has just been erected and the society is in a flourishing condition. In the county there are five organized churches of this denomination with a membership of over four hundred.

Rev. John Beck, of the Reformed church, organized its first society in the county on the 28th of June, 1873, at Grand Prairie. It now has flourishing churches at Hiawatha, Grand Prairie and Fairview, numbering in all about seventy-five members, under the charge of Rev. E. Richards.

Rev. J. H. Ballou (Universalist,) organized a church, Aug., 1867, at Hiawatha, of twenty-one members, and Revs. Ballou, Whitney, Hebbard and Bartlett were its ministers; for two years no regular services have been held.

The Cumberland Presbyterians also had an organization for several years, but of late no meetings have been held.

The Catholics have a church building at Marak's, built in 1869, and a flourishing organization They have also an organization in the western part of the county.

The Episcopal church has been represented in the county since 1866 by Rev. Geo. Turner, who has been actively engaged in advancing the interests of that sect.

All of the churches have been actively engaged in the Sabbath School work. During the summer of 1875 thirty-five sabbath schools were sustained in the county. The reports from Powhattan, Walnut and Hiawatha townships show 1500 persons enrolled in the sabbath schools of those townships. The other five townships have failed to report, but it is safe to say that three thousand persons are connected with the sabbath schools of the county. This embraces at least one-third of the population of the county.

NEWSPAPERS.

The first newspaper in the county, as has been before stated, was published in spring of 1861 by Dr. P. G. Parker. It had a hard struggle for existence and when the office was destroyed by fire the following winter no effort was made to revive it. On the 20th of Aug., 1864, H. P. Stebbins commenced the publication of the Union Sentinel. From a file of this paper, in the possession of Capt. I. J. Lacock, we learn that the First Annual Exhibition of the Brown County Agricultural Society was held Oct. 13th and 14th, 1864, and was considered a decided success. That fall an enterprise was inaugurated to build a wind flouring mill upon an entirely new principle, and during the two succeeding years a large circular building was erected on the north-east portion of the town site. The mill was completed at a cost of nearly $12,000, but was not successful, and at this time no vestige of the building remains. Mr. Stebbins continued the publication of his paper under many difficulties until the 16th of August, 1866, when he transferred it to Ira J. Lacock and J. W. Oberholtzer who at once made a decided improvement in it. The following notice which we find in its issue of Oct. 3d, 1867, gives a good idea of the business houses of Hiawatha at that time, and shows a striking contrast when compared with the business houses of to-day:

The undersigned hereby agree to close their stores and places of business on Friday, Oct. 4t , 1867, it being the second day of the Fair, &c., &c.,
Graves & Stretch,   W. B. Burnett,   Schilling & Meisenheimer,   R. S. Fairchild.

On the 7th of Nov. 1867, Messrs. Lacock & Oberholtzer sold their interest in the Sentinel to David Downer, and retired from the business quite satisfied that publishing a newspaper in a new county required a large amount of labor for a very small compensation. Mr. Downer continued the publication of the Sentinel until Oct. 1st, 1870, when it quietly breathed its last, no notice whatever having been given that it would be discontinued. The probable cause of this sudden death of the Sentinel may be found in the fact, that, on the 30th of April, 1870, A. N. Ruley had commenced the publication of the Hiawatha Dispatch, which still lives to carry its weekly message to its many readers. June, 1874, Davis & Watson commenced the publication of the Brown County Advocate, and on the 23d of July, 1874, Mr. Watson retired and S. L. Roberts succeeded him. About the 20th of Feb., 1875, Mr Davis retired and D. L. Burger became interested in its publication. In Oct., 1875, the name was changed to the Kansas Herald. A. T. McCreary became a member of the firm, remaining till April, 1876, when he retired and Burger & Roberts assumed control again. The Herald is well established.

The following is a list of the names of those who have represented Brown county in the territorial and state legislature, with votes of opposing candidates and members of council ; district comprising Doniphan. Brown. Nemaha, Marshall,Riley and Pottowattomie and all that section of the state west of those counties (being more than one-fourth of all the state,in point of area,) entitled to two members :

Date of Election	Name of Candidate.	No. of Votes
Oct. 5. 1857.	B. Harding F. S. of Wathena	1255
	A J. Mead " " of Manhatten	1255
	Frank J. Marshall Dem.	875
	Henry S. Creal "	875

Nov. 8. 1859. District composed of Brown, Nemaha, Pottowattamie Marshall and Washington,entitled to one member.

	Luther R. Palmer F. S.	476
	Geo. Graham " "	187
	W. W. Guthrie " "	201
	Chas. R. Deming Dem.	182

Dec. 6, 1859. Election held under the Wyandotte constitution, Atchison and Brown comprising the district ; entitled to two Senators.

	John A. Martin Rep.	910
	H. R. Dutton "	925
	Samuel W. Wade Dem.	620
	G. O. Chase "	676

Nov. 5, 1861. Election to fill vacancies. John A. Martin having been appointed postmaster and H. R. Dutton elected State Treasurer.

	W. B. Barnett Rep.	1284
	John J. Ingalls "	814
	Geo. W. Bowman Rep.	705
Nov. 4. 1862.	Brown and Nemaha comprising the district.	
	Byron Sperry Rep.	632
Nov. 8, 1864.	Samuel A. Speer Rep.	475
	James A. Pope "	251
Nov 6, 1866.	George Graham "	757
	J. E. Smith Dem.	224
Nov. 3, 1868.	Albert G. Speer Rep.	1188
	J. Martin Dem.	489
Nov. 8. 1870.	Jos. Cracraft Ind. Rep.	988
	W. B. Slosson "	901
Nov. 5, 1872.	E. N. Morrill "	2196
	J. S. Tyler Lib. "	732
Nov 3, 1874.	J M. Miller "	1485
	Jos. Cracraft Reform	1219

| Date of Election | Name of Candidate. | No. of votes |

Oct. 5, 1857. Members of House of Representatives. Brown and Nemaha entitled to one member.
                                  E. N. Merrill F. S.   283
                                  E. M. Hubbard Dem.   102
Oct. 4, 1858.   Geo. Graham Rep.   129
                                  H. H. Patterson Dem.   73
                                  H Sutherland Rep.   28
Nov. 8, 1859. Brown county being entitled to one member.
                                  H. R. Dutton Rep.   232
                                  A. B. Anderson Rep.   60
Dec. 6, 1859. Election under the Wyandotte Constitution. Atchison and Brown being one District entitled to six members. The vote of Atchison county was not returned to the Secretary of State. Ira H. Smith and Geo. E. Irwin were the candidates from Brown county, the former receiving in this county 175 votes, the latter 168 votes. Atchison county also gave Mr. Smith a majority and he was consequently elected.
Nov. 6, 1860.   W. W. Guthrie Rep.   261
                                  Ira J. Lacock Dem.   161
Nov. 5, 1861. Atchison and Brown same district.
                                  O. H. McCauley Rep.   888
                                  M. C. Willis Dem.   435
Nov. 4, 1862. Brown county being a single district.
                                  Ira J. Lacock Rep.   93
                                  D. K. Babbit   "   6
Nov. 3, 1863. Brown county being entitled to two members
               11th Dist. Ira J. Lacock Rep.   115
                 "   "   Lewis C Dunn Rep.   62
                12th   "   Geo. E. Irwin   "   73
                 "   "   M. L. Sawin   "   45
Nov. 8, 1864. 11th   "   N. P. Rawlings   "   119
                 "   "   R. B. Ransom   "   93
                12th   "   D. Sutherland   "   87
                 "   "   J. S. Tyler   "   61
Nov. 2, 1865. 11th   "   Ira J. Lacock   "   143
                12th   "   C. E. Parker   "   110
                 "   "   J. M. Meredith Dem.   44
Nov. 6, 1866. 11th   "   M. C. Willis, Rep.   192
                 "   "   J. W. Oberholtzer, Rep.   114
                12th   "   C. E. Parker,   "   158
                 "   "   Robt. Rhea, Dem.   9

Date of Election	Name of Candidate.	No. of votes
Nov. 5, 1867		
	11th Dist. E. Bierer, Rep.	217
	" " Ira J. Lacock, Rep.	133
	12th " John Downs. "	185
	" " J. S. Tyler "	29
Nov. 3, 1868		
	11th Dist. M. B. Bowers, Rep.	428
	" " Sam'l Smouse. Dem.	130
	12th " Geo. E. Erwin, Rep.	130
	" " John S. Tyler, "	119
	" " John Meredith, Dem,	42
Nov. 2, 1869		
	11th Dist. J. F. Babbit, Rep.	317
	" " E. Bierer Dem.	113
	12th " A. Curtis Rep.	102
	" " D. L. Anderson Rep.	56
Nov. 8, 1870		
	11th Dist. J. F. Babbit Rep.	225
	" " A. G. Speer "	132
	" " Chas. Knabb Dem.	201
	12th " C. E. Parker Rep.	196
	" " G. E. Irwin "	6
Nov. 7, 1871.	Brown county entitled to one member.	
	C. F. Bowron Rep.	747
	H. A. Parsons Dem.	315
Nov. 5, 1872		
	C. F. Bowron Rep.	1122
	B. F. Killey Lib. Rep.	351
Nov. 4, 1873		
	Jos. D Hardy Ref. Rep.	922
	John G. Spenser "	467
Nov. 3, 1874		
	M. C. Willis Rep.	699
	Jos. D. Hardy Ref. Rep.	641
Nov. —, 1875		
	J. P. Davis Rep.	1192
	J. P. Mulhollen Dem.	225

The following tables give the names of candidates for county offices with vote cast at each election since 1858:

ELECTION HELD NOV. 8TH., 1859.

Name of Office	Name of Candidate	No. of votes
Sheriff	John H. Schenck	237
"	A. M. Gifford	21
Registrar of Deeds	Henry Woodward	186
" " "	David Peebles	113
County Treasurer	Geo. J. Englehart	169
" "	Sam. W. Wade	120
Probate Judge	Benj. F. Killey	281
County Clerk	Henry Graves	287
Prosecuting Attorney	Joel G. Kelsey	238
County Surveyor	Ira H. Smith	137
Co. Supt. of Pub. Inst.	James. H. Stanley	261
Coroner	Andrew J. Selleg	261

ELECTION HELD DEC. 6TH, 1859.
(Under Wyandotte Constitution.)

Name of Office	Name of Candidate	No. of votes
Probate Judge	E. Plankington	346
District Clerk	H. L. Dean	176
" "	Joel G. Kelsey	154
Co. Supt. Pub. Inst.	Joseph Paschal	261
" " " "	M. C. Willis	93

ELECTION HELD MAR. 26TH, 1860.

Name of Office			Name of Candidate	No. of votes
County Commiss'r. 1st Dist.			W. B. Barnett	165
" "	"	"	L. C. Dunn	48
"	"	2d	I. B. Hoover	158
"	"	" "	Noah Hanson	49
"	"	" "	W. H. Piatt	17
"	"	3d	James Round	202
County Assessor			E. A. Spooner	115
"	"		Joseph Paschal	60

HISTORY OF

Name of Office	Name of Candidate	No. of votes
County Assessor	L. C. Dunn	13
" "	John Maxwell	27

ELECTION HELD NOV. 6TH, 1860.

Name of Office	Name of Candidate	No. of votes
County Commissioner	James Round	249
" "	William Vassar	261
" "	Lewis C. Dunn	285
" "	M. C. Willis	165
" "	W. S. McLaughlin	133
" "	W. C. Foster	163
County Assessor	E. A. Spooner	278
" "	H. C. Gregg	143
Co. Supt. of Schools	G. G. Rice	265
" "	T. Kemper	150
County Clerk	E. L. Pound	260
" "	J. W. Oberholtzer	159
County Attorney	E. W. Plankington	264
" "	W. G. Sargent	154
Coroner	Sam. W. Wade	142

ELECTION HELD NOV. —, 1861.

Name of Office	Name of Candidate	No. of votes
County Commissioner	Noah Hanson	268
" "	James Round	262
" "	Thos. Ellis	266
Sheriff	I. B. Hoover	265
Probate Judge	W. W. Guthrie	241
" "	Amasa Owen	16
County Treasurer	Geo. J. Englehart	200
" "	Sam. Speer	72
County Clerk	E. L. Pound	269
Registrar of Deeds	David Peebles	250
County Assessor	W. J. Hart	169
" "	G. G. Rice	95
County Surveyor	E. H. Niles	266
Supt. of Common Schools	G. G. Rice	254
Coroner	Orville Root	264

BROWN COUNTY.

ELECTION HELD NOV. 4TH, 1862.

Name of Office	Name of Candidate	No. of votes
District Clerk	Joel G. Kelsey	222
Probate Judge	Geo. G. Rice	164
" "	B. F. Killey	95
Co. Supt. Public Inst.	Geo. G. Rice	249

ELECTION HELD NOV. 3d, 1863.

Name of Office	Name of Candidate	No. of votes
County Treasurer	E. L. Pound	299
County Clerk	E. A. Spooner	298
Sheriff	H. M. Robinson	267
"	Chas. Fox	7
Registrar of Deeds	J. W. Oberholtzer	301
County Assessor	D. K. Babbit	268
" "	—— Sawyer	3
County Surveyor	Elbridge Chase	302
Coroner	Wm. H. Jones	265
"	R. H. Bollinger	2
County Commissioner	M. C. Willis	218
" "	Isaiah P. Winslow	278
" "	Isaiah Travis	300
" "	R. H. Bollinger	78

ELECTION HELD NOV. 8TH., 1864.

Name of Office	Name of Candidate	No. of votes
District Clerk	Joel G. Kelsey	237
Probate Judge	E. A. Spooner	313
County Attorney	B. F. Killey	292
Co. Supt. Public Inst.	Noah Hanson	310

ELECTION HELD NOV. 6TH, 1865.

Name of Office	Name of Candidate	No. of votes
County Commis'r, 1st Dist	E. S. Barnum	116
" " " "	Isaiah P. Winslow	214
" " 2d "	W. C. Meyers	71
" " " "	E. A. Spooner	263
" " 3d Dist	John Maglott	148
" " " "	M. C. Willis	178

Name of Office.	Name of Candidate.	No. of votes
County Treasurer	W. B. Barnett	191
" "	Harvey Seburn	157
County Clerk	Joel G. Kelsey	309
" "	C. F. Bowron	3
Sheriff	H. M. Robinson	134
Registrar of Deeds	J. W. Oberholtzer	353
County Assessor	A. D. Westerfield	340
" "	A. J. Owen	19
County Surveyor	E. H. Niles	340
Coroner	Geo. W. Parker	346

ELECTION HELD NOV. 6TH, 1866.

Name of Office	Name of Candidate	No. of votes
District Clerk	E. N. Morrill	437
Co. Supt. Public Inst.	Noah Hanson	457
Probate Judge	E. A. Spooner	473
County Attorney	B. F. Killey	226
" "	E. Bierer	76
" "	D. K. Babbit	21

ELECTION HELD NOV. 5TH., 1867.

Name of Office	Name of Candidate	No. of votes
County Treasurer	W. B. Barnett	603
County Clerk	E. N. Morrill	558
Sheriff	I. N. Seaman	267
"	Eli Moser	309
Registrar of Deeds	J. K. Klinefelter	196
" " "	J. W. Oberholtzer	384
County Assessor	J. K. Bunn	227
" "	D. K. Babbit	366
County Surveyor	J. O. Shannon	233
" "	E. H. Niles	355
County Commis'r, 1st Dist.	M. B. Bowers	220
" " " "	John Walters	337
" " 2d "	Jacob J. Weltmer	552
" " 3d "	S. W. Wade	129
" " " "	Theodore Schecker	122
" " " "	J. K. Dickinson	209

Vote in Brown County cast for the different county offices on Nov. 3d. 1868. Whole number of votes cast 873

Name of Office	Name of Candidate	No. of votes
Clerk of Dist. Court	E. N. Morrill	684
" " " "	David Glenn	178
Supt. of Pub. Inst.	Noah Hanson	667
" " " "	H. Hall	193
County Attorney	B. F. Killey	677
" "	J. J. Miles	179
Probate Judge	D. K. Babbit	674
" "	Joseph Hall	181

Vote for 1869. Whole number of votes cast 645

Name of Office	Name of Candidate	No. of votes
County Commissioner	C. F. Bowron	598
" "	John S. Tyler	569
" "	Martin C. Willis	470
" "	D. J. Parks	128
County Treasurer	A. McLaughlin	403
" "	H. M. Robinson	225
County Clerk	E. N. Morrill	477
" "	D. Downer	90
" "	E. A. Spooner	11
Registrar of Deeds	J. W. Oberholtzer	339
" " "	J. K. Klinefelter	228
Sheriff	J. E. Bowers	172
"	I. N. Seaman	116
"	J. K. Klinefelter	103
"	B. B. Munn	88
"	J A. Wilson	60
	N. Cardray	49
"	Geo. E. Selleg	31
County Surveyor	S. W. Aldrich	614
Coroner	S. Wilkinson	581
"	A. Kimball	13

Vote for Nov. 8, 1870. Whole number of votes cast 817

Name of Office	Name of Candidate	No. of v tes
Clerk of District Court	H J. Aten	266
" " " "	S. E. Erwin	215
County Attorney	A. R. May	540

Name of Office	Name of Candidate	No. of votes
County Attorney	F. M. Keith	231
Probate Judge	D. K. Babbit	732
Supt. of Pub. Inst.	R. C. Chase	755
Vote for Nov. 7, 1871.	Whole number of votes cast	1109

Name of Office	Name of Candidate	No. of votes
County Commissioner	B. F. Partch	652
" "	M. B. Bowers	635
" "	A. M. Hough	748
" "	H. S. Lytle	323
" "	T. Schecker	374
" "	Wm. Hewitt	353
County Treasurer	A. McLaughlin	794
" "	A. Schilling	261
County Clerk	E. N. Morrill	766
" "	E. Bierer	276
Sheriff	B. F. McCoy	657
"	G. B. Jones	372
Registrar of Deeds	A. R. Platt	554
" " "	J. A. Pope	441
County Surveyor	S. E. Erwin	748
" "	C. B. Ellis	307
Coroner	S. Wilkinson	756
"	S. Smouse	287
Vote for Nov. 5, 1872.	Whole number of votes cast	1525

Name of Office	Name of Candidate	No. of votes
Clerk of Dist. Court	Henry Anderson	1114
" " " "	J. F. Roehm	400
County Attorney	Ira J. Lacock	1075
" "	Henry A. Parsons	387
Probate Judge	D. K. Babbit	1105
" "	G. Amann	383
County Commissioner	H. F. Macy	1124
" "	Adam Schilling	384
Supt. of Pub. Inst.	R. C. Chase	1125
" " " "	O. Fountain	348
Vote for Nov. 4, 1873.	Whole number of votes cast	1406

Name of Office	Name of Candidate	No. of votes
County Treasurer	Harvey Seburn	953
" "	H. F. Macy	438

BROWN COUNTY.

Name of Office	Name of Candidate	No. of votes
County Clerk	Henry Isely	847
" "	Jacob Reasoner	548
Registrar of Deeds	F D. Howlette	880
" " "	A. R. Platt	508
Sheriff	Albert Rokes	716
"	B. F. McCoy	480
"	C. H. Orth	194
County Surveyor	S. E. Erwin	877
" "	L. P. Hazen	518
Coroner	H. Honnell	888
"	J. M. Castle	503
Co. Commis'r 1st Dist.	C. A. Saylor	286
" " " "	L. P. Winslow	135
" " 2d "	A. Walters	275
" " " "	O. Fountain	220
" " 3d "	Jno. McCrerey	315
" " " "	C. L. Carroll	146

Vote for Nov. 3, 1874. Whole number of votes cast 1373

Name of Office	Name of Candidate	No. of votes
Clerk of Dist. Court	J. W. Oberholtzer	782
" " " "	David L. Burger	571
County Attorney	F. M. Keith	736
" "	Jas. Falloon	609
Supt of Pub. Inst.	R. C. Chase	779
" " " "	D. C. Nutting	566
Probate Judge	T. B. Dickason	760
" "	N. P. Rawlings	594

Vote for Nov. 2, 1875. Whole number of votes cast 1482

Name of Office	Name of Candidate	No. of votes
County Treasurer	James B. Allison	675
" "	Harvey Seburn	796
County Clerk	Jacob Reasoner	630
" "	Henry Isely	839
Registrar of Deeds	E. D. Benner	733
" " "	Jacob F. Roehm	699
Sheriff	C. H. Lawrence	700
"	Albert Rokes	523
"	P. C. McGilvary	231

Name of Office	Name of Candidate	No. of votes
Sheriff	A. J. Comstock	2
County Surveyor	H. P. Kinney	829
" "	J. O. Shannon	597
Coroner	Wm. Shirley	888
"	W. A. Turner	528
County Commis'r 1st Dist.	C. F. Bowron	230
" " " "	S. Sherman	183
" " 2d "	Alfred Walters	463
" " " "	R. McCartney	38
" " 3d "	C. L. Carroll	313
" " " "	Theo. Scheeker	164

COUNTY LINES.

The Legislature of 1868 changed the county lines by transferring townships five, ranges fifteen and sixteen from Brown to Jackson county. This is the only change that has ever been made in the boundaries, and leaves the county just twenty-four miles square.

RISE AND FALL OF THE HIAWATHA CLUB.

COMPILED FOR THE AUTHOR BY A. R. MAY, ESQ., CITY ATTORNEY.

During the year 1875 the City Council refused to grant any dram shop or saloon licenses in the city, and no intoxicating liquors were sold excepting such as may have been sold in the drug stores, until about October 7th, 1875, when there was a movement originated by a few persons, ostensibly for the purpose of forming a Beer Club for the purpose of social enjoyment, but in reality for the purpose of opening and maintaining a dram shop in violation of law, and evading the license laws of the city.

A petition was circulated and numerously signed, bearing the following heading:

"We, the undersigned, hereby agree, to and with "each other, to form and arrange a club for the pur- "pose of social enjoyment, said club to have its rooms "in the city of Hiawatha, and to be known as 'The "Hiawatha Club.' Dated this 7th day of Oct., 1875."

About the same time, and probably on the same day, Fred W. Rohl and Henry Stauff, two persons then living about eight miles south of town, opened the building situated on the east half of lot No. 91, on Oregon St., commonly called the Billiard Hall or Corn Exchange, and owned by J.W.Pottenger,as the headquarters of the Hiawatha Club. They immediately and almost daily shipped large quantities of beer and liquors to said room,and the same was handed out to their customers, by said Rohl and Stauff, and drank on the premises, the customers paying therefor with printed tickets or checks, bought from Rohl and Stauff at five cents per ticket or check, one ticket procuring a glass of beer and two a drink of whisky, the more fancy drinks requiring more in proportion. Afterwards, at a meeting held by the club, on October 13th, 1875, the club adopted a constitution and rules of order for their government, which among other things provided that the officers of the association should consist of a Prsident, Vice President, Secretary, Treasurer and five Trustees, who together should form the Board of Management, to manage the affairs of the association. That the officers should be elected annually. That stated meetings should be held monthly. That members should be proposed one week before election, elected by ballot, receiving not less than ten affirmative to each negative vote, and after election each member should pay an entrance fee of 25 cents. The constitution also provided that each member must procure tickets from the treasurer for refreshments before the same were partaken of.

In order to do away with the necessity of being formally proposed and ballotted for as a member, however, the constitution wisely and sagaciously provided "that any member might invite gentlemen to the rooms of the association for a single day on registering his own name with that of the visitor in a book kept for that purpose, thus securing to the tired and weary wayfarer a convenient oasis of refreshment.

The house committee was charged with the duty of appointing the employees and regulating the price of articles furnished to members in the house, and while Messrs. Rohl and Stauff at their trial testified that they were appointed by the house committee to fill their respective stations, yet they had reluctantly to admit that they neglected to fix any compensation for their services, which to the mind of the Court did not seem to be very consistent with their defense, that they were not the proprietors of the establishment and running it for their own benefit and private gain, but simply as the paid employees of a lawful organization.

Other rules were adopted as standing rules, one of which was, that the house should be open at 9 o'clock in the morning DAILY for the reception of members, and close at 12 o'clock in the evening, but the rule was not to influence members then actually in the house in respect to their departure.

This state of affairs lasted until the 15th of October, when H. J. Aten, Mayor of the City, issued his written order to G. T. Woodmansee, the City Marshal, commanding him to take charge of and close up said building, as a place dangerous to the peace and quiet of the city, and to keep the same closed until Saturday night, October 16th, at 12 o'clock, P. M., which order the Marshal promptly executed.

Early on the following Monday morning Rohl and Stauff opened the building again and prosecuted their business of selling beer and liquor as they had done before, and continued to do so until October 20th, when Mayor Aten issued a second order to the City Marshal commanding him to close the building, and keep it closed for the space of three days from that date, which order the Marshal immediately attempted to execute, but was forcibly ejected from the premises by Rohl and Stauff and several other members of the club.

He made one or two more attempts afterwards to execute the same, but finding the door locked and guarded every time that he made the attempt, he summoned as a posse, Thomas McLaughlin, J. K. Klinefelter and G. E. Selleg.

They proceeded to the room, broke open the door,

forcibly ejected the occupants and locked the building up.

Shortly thereafter, Rohl and Stauff, and others, broke open the building, entered the same, and prosecuted their business the same as before.

Immediately after their expulsion from the building Fred W. Rohl made affidavit before W. J. Richardson, J. P., and procured a warrant for the arrest of G. T. Woodmansee and his said posse on a charge of riot.

The case was prosecuted before W. J. Richardson, J. P., by James Falloon and County Attorney, F. M. Keith, for the State, and the prisoners were defended by the City Attorney, A. R. May, Ira J. Lacock and C. E. Berry. The jury promptly brought in a verdict of not guilty and found that the prosecution was without cause. The Justice thereupon discharged the prisoners, and taxed the costs of prosecution to the prosecuting witness, F. W. Rohl.

By this time matters had assumed quite a serious aspect: the club members declaring that the city had no right to interfere in their business, and that they would resist any further attempt at interference even to the shedding of blood, and stating that they were advised by their counsel to do so. The city authorities, on the other hand, were determined that the ordinances of the city should be enforced at all hazards and at any cost.

On Nov. 18th Rohl and Stauff were arrested for a violation of the city ordinances in selling intoxicating liquors in said building, and the case was tried before Police Justice J. P. Mulhollen, on Nov. 22, and resulted in the conviction of the defendants, and in the imposition of a fine of $50 each on the defendants. From this judgement the defendants appealed to the District Court.

Rohl and Stauff, however, still continued their business, and became even more bold and defiant, stating that no matter how often they would be convicted they would appeal their cases and sell liquor all the same.

By this time, also, the place became an intolerable nuisance by reason of the boisterous and indecent behavior of the drunken people, day and night, in and around the building, the same being on the most public street and in the business portion of the city.

On November 27th, Rohl and Stauff were again arrested on the charge of keeping and maintaining a common public nuisance in said building, and on trial before the Police Judge Dec., 2d, [were] convicted of keeping a nuisance and the premises adjudged a nuisance and ordered to be abated, and defendants ordered to pay the costs. From this judgment the defendants also promptly appealed, and kept on selling liquor in the building as they had previously done.

Thereupon, on or about the 15th day of Dec., 1875, the Mayor issued his writ to the City Marshal, (as the ordinance provided,) reciting the aforesaid judgment and ordering him to abate said nuisance.

After several ineffectual attempts by the Marshal to enforce said writ, being met by Rohl and Stauff with drawn revolvers and threats that they would shoot him if he attempted to carry the order into effect, he summoned to his aid a large posse of citizens, among whom were S. P. Gaskill, A. A. Holmes, R. C. Chase, George D. Blair, W. S. Bristol, J. C. Thomas, A. McLaughlin, and others, who, besides some volunteers numbering in all about twenty men, early on the morning of Dec. 25th, 1875, repaired to the saloon armed with revolvers, shot guns and sabres, forcibly ejected Henry Stauff, Rohl retreating in some disorder, emptied all the liquors found in the establishment, captured the books and papers of the club, and with the billiard tables and furniture barricaded the doors. They then stationed guards on the outside and inside of the building, all heavily armed, and kept it guarded until some ten or twelve days thereafter when the question of the occupancy of the building was settled by injunction proceedings in the District Court. Immediately after the building was occupied by the Marshal and his posse, Rohl and Stauff sent word into the country of the fact to numerous members of the club, who, to the number of several hundred, flocked to town, some being armed, breathing vengeance against the authorities and threatening to make an attack on the Marshal and his force and re-take the building.

Throughout the entire day and the greater portion of the night hundreds of the members of the club and their sympathizers congregated in the vicinity of the building, blaspheming and threatening to break into the building by force, and the citizens generally believed that an attempt of that kind would be made, but no actual attempt was made.

While these misguided rioters showed by their acts and deeds the intensity of their feelings at the invasion of their cherished rights,—the right to sell, buy and drink intoxicating liquors without regard to the laws of the land,—yet they quailed before the determined countenances of the men who guarded the building, and beyond venting their feelings in language, nothing further was done.

Matters remained thus for several days, when Rohl and Stauff served a notice on the city that they would apply for an injunction before Judge Hubbard, at Atchison. The city immediately served notice on

Rohl and Stauff that it would at the same time and place apply for an injunction on its part against them, filed its cross petition, and on Dec. 31st, 1875, obtained a temporary injunction against Rohl and Stauff, conditioned that on filing a bond in the sum of $200, Rohl and Stauff should be restrained from interfering with the premises in any manner whatever, for the space of five days, when the court would hear the matter further at Troy.

Rohl and Stauff never filed their petition and did not appear at Atchison. The city gave the required bond, and at the time fixed, appeared at Troy. This time Rohl and Stauff appeared, but instead of asking for the injunction on their part, sought to prevent the city from obtaining one against them, on the grounds that they never filed their petition for an injunction, and that the city could not maintain its application on a cross petition to their petition which was not filed, and not pressed; and also, because the title of the city's petition should be changed so as to make it plaintiff instead of defendant.

Judge Hubbard overruled these several objections and held that the service of notice on the city by Rohl and Stauff of their intention to apply for an injunction against the city, gave it the right to prevent in the manner it did; and the case was then fully presented on both sides, numerous affidavits being presented. After a full hearing Judge Hubbard, on Jan. 6th, 1876, granted an injunction, in favor of the city, restraining Rohl and Stauff from using the premises for the sale of or keeping of liquors of any kind therein, until the April term of our court, on condition that the city file a bond of $1000 which they immediately did; also an order, that upon the filing by Rohl and Stauff of a bond in the sum of $200, the city should turn over the building and books, papers, &c., captured in the same on the memorable 25th of Dec. Rohl and Stauff never filed their bond, but the city immediately turned over to J. W. Pottenger, who demanded the possession of the building, the same, and after obtaining copies of all the captured books, papers, &c., turned the same over to Rohl and Stauff.

Thus ended the Hiawatha Beer Club, they never afterwards establishing any other place of business in this city for the sale of liquor. Rohl and Stauff, however, as individuals, applied to the courts, and on Feb. 10th, 1876, each of them filed suits, individually, against H. J. Aten, G. T. Woodmansee, W. S. Bristol, S. R. Gaskill, R. C. Chase, A. A. Holmes, Wm. Clement and J. C. Thomas, for damages done to their persons and feelings, Rohl claiming $5000 damages, and Stauff a like amount, and also claiming $100 additional for cigars which he alleged the defendents destroyed. Both these petitions were demurred and the demurrers sustained; but leave was granted by the court to file amended petitions. Before this time, Dec. 13th, 1875, Henry Stauff brought suit in the District Court against G. T. Woodmansee for $500 damages for ejecting him from the building. On Dec. 25th, 1875, Henry Stauff and Murry Stanley were arrested on a state warrant charged with threatening to commit a breach of the peace on R. C. Chase. There was no appearance made against the parties. On the same day S. P. Gaskill, W. S. Bristol, A. A. Holmes J. C. Thomas, A. McLaughlin, B. F. Partch, G. T. Woodmansee, Geo. M. Blair, Wm. Clement, J. K. Klinefelter, R. Chase, A. G. Speer, Thurston Chase, L. S. Herbert, A. Rokes and Rev. C. L. Shackelford were arrested on oath of Henry Stauff, charged with committing an assault and battery, &c., on said Stauff, which case was heard before G. W. Seaman, J. P., and the information quashed. Both these last prosecutions arose out of the Beer Club business.

Shortly after the adjournment of the April term of court, 1876, Rohl and Stauff gave themselves up voluntarily to the Sheriff, stating that they could not pay their fines and that he would have to take charge of them. He kept them in the city calaboose, which was broken into by their friends one night, and the prisoners liberated; but it was repaired and they were put back. After staying in the calaboose for several days, Reverends Shackelford and Liggett interested themselves in their behalf, visited them in their cell, and the result was that the mayor and city council were petitioned by Rohl and Stauff to remit their fines and discharge them, they, Rohl and Stauff, to pay all costs and dismiss all suits by them against the citizens, and the city to dismiss all proceedings against them. This was done, and the money for paying the costs mostly raised by subscription, the larger part being contributed by the temperance people.

CONCLUSION.

In conclusion we desire to compare briefly the Brown county of to-day with the Brown county of 1855. The first tax collected in the county was for the year 1856, and the total tax for that year amounted to $52. The taxes of 1875 amounted to $83,144. The first assessment roll of the county now in existence is that of 1857, which shows a taxable property in the county of $8,078, of which $1400 was for four slaves. The assessment roll of 1876 shows a taxable property of $3,162,690. In 1855 the first farms were opened and the first crops planted. Until that time no plow had ever disturbed the virgin soil. In 1876 175,040 acres were under cultivation, an increase of 26,000 acres over 1875. In 1875, after thousands of acres of crops had been destroyed by grasshoppers, there were raised in the county 200,000 bushels of small grain, 2,750,000 bushels of corn, 1,000,000 lbs of broom corn, 50,000 bushels of potatoes, and smaller quantities of sweet potatoes, flax, sorghum and millet. The total products of the county for that year being valued at $1,162,820. The crop of 1876 will be much larger and the money value will be considerably more. In 1857 there were 125 head of horses and 684 head of cattle. In 1876 there were 6194 head of horses and 17,184 head of cattle. In 1857 there were no animals to sell for slaughter and very few slaughtered for home consumption.

In 1875 the value of animals slaughtered and sold for slaughter was $200,000. In 1857 the first fruit trees were planted in the county. To-day there are 115,645 apple trees growing, of which 18,794 are bearing fruit. There are 1371 pear trees, 155,269 peach trees, and 19,080 cherry trees, now, in good condition. This would make an average of 32 fruit trees to each man, woman and child in the county. This does not include the trees in nurseries covering 377 acres and numbering millions. In addition to this there are 25 acres of vineyards in the county and an immense quantity of the smaller fruits. Who can estimate the quantity of fruit that will be produced in the county in 1886? The sales of butter and eggs for 1875 were nearly $40,000. In 1854 the first white man settled in the county; to-day there is a population of 9000. There were no schools and no churches; to-day there are seventy-five schools taught in the county at an expense of $30,000 per annum, and twenty church organizations are actively engaged in educating the people up to a higher life.

The future promises to be a bright one for our county. With a soil and climate unsurpassed in the United States; with an enterprising, honest, industrious and temperate class of settlers, the future prosperity of the county is assured. In only one respect is Brown county unlike the other counties of the state. It has NO WHISKY SALOON and NO JAIL! It will never need the former; may it never have any use for the latter.

THE END.

www.ingramcontent.com/pod-product-compliance
Lightning Source LLC
Chambersburg PA
CBHW020324090426
42735CB00009B/1400